THE ENCYCLOPEDIA OF
MUSICAL INSTRUMENTS
STRINGED INSTRUMENTS

Produced by Carlton Books Limited
20 Mortimer Street
London, W1N 7RD

Text and Design copyright © Carlton Books Limited 2001

First published in hardback edition in 2001 by Chelsea House Publishers, a subsidiary of
Haights Cross Communications. Printed and bound in Dubai.

3 5 7 9 8 6 4 2

The Chelsea House World Wide Web address is http://www.chelseahouse.com

Library of Congress Cataloging-in-Publication Data applied for

Woodwind and Brass Instruments ISBN: 0-7910-6091-8
Stringed Instruments ISBN: 0-7910-6092-6
Percussion and Electronic Instruments ISBN: 0-7910-6093-4
Keyboard Instruments and Ensembles ISBN: 0-7910-6094-2
Non-Western and Obsolete Instruments ISBN: 0-7910-6095-0

THE ENCYCLOPEDIA OF
MUSICAL INSTRUMENTS

STRINGED INSTRUMENTS

ROBERT DEARLING

Chelsea House Publishers

Philadelphia

THE ENCYCLOPEDIA OF
MUSICAL INSTRUMENTS

STRINGED INSTRUMENTS

Woodwind and Brass Instruments

Percussion and Electronic Instruments

Keyboard Instruments and Ensembles

Non-Western and Obsolete Instruments

7940

CONTENTS

Stringed Instruments

STRINGED INSTRUMENTS ARE those which produce their sound from a vibrating string set in motion by bowing, plucking or striking it. The first category includes not just the violin family, which has become the foundation of the modern orchestra, but also the viols which developed alongside them, plus a whole range of instruments whose existence has been more transitory. All of these rely on the player's non-bowing hand to stop the vibrating string at different points in order to raise its pitch. This is also a feature of many plucked instruments such as the guitar, although the harp provides the most notable exception. Most of the commoner struck stringed instruments really belong to the category of either keyboard or non-Western instruments.

THE ASSUMPTION OF THE VIRGIN (C. 1500), BY PIETRO DI CRISTOFERO VANUCCI, SHOWING ANGELS PLAYING HARP AND VIOLA DA BRACCIO.

VIOL

It is a common misconception that the viols preceded and evolved into the modern string family. Both can trace their ancestry back at least as far as the closing years of the 15th century and earlier paintings reveal evidence that in the Middle Ages two distinct types of bowed instruments were recognized, those played on the arm or shoulder (*da braccio*) and those held between the legs (*da gamba*). Nevertheless, it was the viol which first emerged as a distinct instrumental type and which remained the most important of the bowed strings throughout the Renaissance period.

⸷ Construction

The structure and design of the viol continued to evolve well into the Baroque, all the while retaining a number of features which distinguished the instrument from the upstart violin, principally the flat back and sloping shoulders. Its fingerboard was fretted like that of a guitar and its bow held with an underhand grip, not overhand as with the violin, viola or cello, thus enabling the player to control the tension of the hair with the middle finger. Moreover, it had between five and seven strings, with six being by far the commonest number. Another characteristic shared with the guitar is its tuning in fourths with the interval of a third between the third and fourth strings of six-stringed instruments.

A VIOL BY THE VENETIAN MAKER ANTONIO CICILIANO, DATED C. 1600.

Both viols and violins are already mentioned in the very first printed treatise on musical instruments, Sebastian Virdung's *Musica getutscht* (1511), in which a nine-string instrument is described. Eighteen years later five- and six-string viols are described in Martin Agricola's *Musica instrumentalis deudsch*. But the most important 16th-century document to discuss the instrument is the *Regolo Rubertina*, published by Silvestro Ganassi in 1542. This is the first treatise not only to describe and illustrate the viol but to provide instruction in how it was to be played. Both Agricola and Ganassi refer to the treble (its bass closer in tuning to what we would recognize as the tenor), tenor and bass as being the most important sizes. Ganassi, however, gives for these three instruments the tuning that was to become standard in the later Renaissance and Baroque: the bass pitched an octave lower than the treble and the tenor a fourth higher than the bass (see panel feature).

⸷ In Performance

The viol quickly established itself as a gregarious instrument, well suited to domestic music making. Affluent households would possess a 'chest' of viols as we might today have a piano, and it was considered part of a sound education to be able to take

TYPES OF *Viol*

⸷

PARDESSUS DE VIOLE Pitched a fourth above the treble but often lacks the lowest string, although seven-string instruments tuned like the treble but with an extra top *g"* string are known. A latecomer to the family, it developed in France in the early 18th century and was a popular amateur instrument.

TREBLE VIOL The smallest of the commonly used viols, this generally takes the top line in consort music. The six strings of the Baroque instrument are usually tuned *d, g, c', e', a', d"*.

ALTO VIOL Developed alongside its better known companions but was largely restricted to the occasional appearance in consort music, particularly in England. Ganassi describes it as a small tenor with identical tuning, but by the 17th century it was commonly pitched a whole tone lower than the treble, with some five-stringed examples lacking a top *c"*.

TENOR VIOL Provides the middle voices in consort music but has little solo repertoire. Its commonest tuning is *G, c, f, a, d', g'*; an instrument pitched a tone higher is occasionally found.

LYRA VIOL Can refer to an instrument midway in size between the tenor and bass, but equally used to describe a richly chordal style of solo playing popular in the 17th century.

BASS VIOL Often referred to simply as the viola da gamba. The foundation of the consort, it emerged in the Baroque era as a solo instrument in its own right. Its six strings are generally tuned *D, G, c, e, a, d*, but seven-string instruments with a low *A'* are not uncommon.

GREAT BASS VIOL Can be tuned like the seven-string bass without the top *d*, or with the *c* tuned to *B*.

VIOLONE Pitched an octave below the bass viol and the ancestor of the modern double bass.

one's part in a piece for a group, or consort, of viols. This was particularly true in England which, like France, was slower to succumb to the charms of the violin, which was then gaining ground in Italy. In the Elizabethan and Jacobean periods particularly, pieces in several parts were often deemed 'apt for voices or viols', while a great heritage of purely instrumental music has been bequeathed to us by composers such as William Byrd and Orlando Gibbons.

In England chamber music with viols, or for the 'broken consort' of mixed instruments, remained popular well into the 17th century. Charles I learnt the viol from the younger Alfonso Ferrabosco and maintained his own consort, as did Oliver Cromwell, despite his strict views on public music. Chamber music actually flourished during the Protectorate, with

composers like John Jenkins and William Lawes contributing significantly to the viol's repertoire. It also witnessed the increasing emergence of the bass viol as a solo instrument. In 1659 Christopher Simpson published his enormously successful *The division violist*, giving instruction in the playing of 'divisions' or variations as well as the technique of the viol. Although the Restoration saw the beginning of the decline in the viol's fortunes, it did produce, in Purcell's *Fantasias*, a worthy swansong to a noble tradition. At the same time France was enjoying a golden age of viol playing; the solo music of Marin Marais, Caix d'Hervelois and Antoine Forqueray is central to the player's art. In Germany, too, the late Baroque produced some fine music for the bass viol. Bach wrote three sonatas for the instrument and included it in the sixth

'Brandenburg' concerto as well as numerous choral works. Carl Friedrich Abel, the last of the great viola da gamba virtuosi, was the business partner of Bach's youngest son, Johann Christian, in London.

Although the bass viol probably never became totally obsolete as an amateur instrument, the viols disappeared from concert life during the Classical and Romantic periods. Their modern revival began in the 1890s when the pioneering early music specialist Arnold Dolmetsch gave his first concerts on surviving viols and began to make modern copies. A century later we take it for granted that we can hear the huge viol repertoire played on the instruments for which it was intended. Many fine instruments are also being made or copied from originals. 𝄢

𝒱iol
CONFUSION
✄

The fact that the word viol translates into Italian as viola sometimes causes confusion. True viols are always played between the knees, hence the name viola da gamba ('leg viol'). This can refer to instruments of any size within the family, but is usually reserved for the bass viol (see illustration left). The commonest types of viol are the treble, tenor and bass; see page 47.

A GROUP OF MUSICIANS DEPICTED BY LOUIS LE NAIN (C. 1593–1648). THE PLAYER ON THE LEFT HOLDS A BASS VIOL.

♪VIOLIN

♪ AN EXAMPLE OF A
VIOLIN FROM THE
WORKSHOP OF ONE OF
THE GREATEST MAKERS OF
STRINGED INSTRUMENTS,
NICOLO AMATI —
SEE FEATURE

IF YOU STAND beneath the dome of Saronno Cathedral in Italy and look upwards, your eye will be caught by the splendid frescoes painted by Gaudenzio Ferrari. They date from around 1535 and show angels playing instruments, among them the earliest known collective representation of the modern string family of violin, viola and cello. They appear to have three strings, but by the mid-century four-stringed instruments were already known, as both written and pictorial evidence shows. Much of this evidence confirms that, although the violin family soon found its way across Europe, it was in Italy that it could claim to have been born. Some of the earliest true violins to survive come from northern Italy, chiefly the Milanese areas of Brescia and Cremona, and Venice, a part of the world which was to maintain pre-eminence in violin making for the next two centuries. The first known maker was Andreas Amati, the founder of the celebrated Cremona school, who was born there some time at the beginning of the 16th century.

The Italian *violino* simply means 'little viola', but there is no evidence to support the notion that the viola predates its smaller sibling. Confusion is apt to arise because *viola* is the Italian for 'viol'. Early references to both viola and violin often specify that they are *da braccio*, probably to differentiate them from the viols, which were never played 'on the arm'.

❧ Construction

Although the violin has undergone several modifications since the 16th century, its structure has remained essentially the same. The front (or belly), the back and the middle section (or ribs) are made as separate pieces from a soft wood, such as spruce. The bottom, top and corners of the rib section are reinforced by blocks. The belly is pierced by two sound holes shaped like a cursive 'f', and a bass bar is attached to its underside, running parallel to the lower strings, its position determined by one foot of the bridge which supports the strings. Underneath the opposite foot of the bridge is the soundpost, which runs vertically towards the back of the instrument. At one end of the neck, which is made separately of a harder wood, is the scroll, containing the tuning pegs. The strings run from these across the fingerboard, placed on top of the neck, over the bridge to the tail piece which is looped around the end button. The start of the fingerboard is marked by the nut. The inlaid decoration around the edges of the belly and back is known as 'purfling'.

The earliest bows of the violin family seem to have been modelled on those of the viol. The wood was convex and the frog which held the horsehair at the end nearest the player was fixed, leaving the fingers of the right hand to vary the tension. Violin bows of the 16th and early 17th centuries could be as short as 35cm (14 inches), particularly those used in dance music, one area where the violin quickly found a niche.

For four-stringed instruments the modern *g*, *d', a', e"* tuning had been established by the late

♪ AS THIS ILLUSTRATION SHOWS, THE
EARLIEST VIOLINS WERE NOT HELD
ON THE SHOULDER AS THEY ARE
NOWADAYS. NOTE ALSO THE BOW, WHICH
IS SHORT AND CONVEX.

Famous Violin Makers

❉

THE AMATIS
Italy's early predominance in the making of string instruments lasted for well over two centuries. The earliest recorded name is that of Andrea Amati (c. 1505–80), the Cremonese founder of a whole dynasty of makers, or *luthiers*. He was followed by his two sons, Antonio (c.1538–95) and Girolamo (c.1561–1630). The latter's son Nicolo (1596–1684) was the most illustrious of the Amatis. Some of his violins are characterized by their large size compared to those of his father and uncle and by their correspondingly more powerful tone. Instruments by Nicolo Amati can be recognized from their label signed *Nicolaus Amati Cremonens, Hieronimi filius Antonii nepos* ('Nicolo Amati of Cremona, son of Girolamo and nephew of Antonio'). Nicolo was also the teacher of Guarneri and Stradivari. His son Girolamo II (1649–1740) was the last of the dynasty. Although influenced by Stradivari, his workmanship rarely equalled that of his mentor or his father.

THE GUARNERIS
The head of Cremona's second great violin-making dynasty, Andreas Guarneri (c.1625–98), trained under Nicolo Amati and lived in his house as an apprentice. Instruments from this period are labelled *alumnus* ('pupil'); from 1655 this changes to *ex alumnis* ('from the school

of'). His son Pietro (1655–1720) worked first at Cremona and thereafter at Mantua. Like his father, he often designated himself *sub titolo Sanctae Theresiae* ('under the label of St. Teresa'). His brother Giuseppe (1666–c.1740) remained in and eventually inherited his father's workshop; his own son Pietro II (1695–1762) moved to Venice and is distinguished from his uncle by the epithet *Pietro di Venezia*. The most celebrated Guarneri violins are those of Giuseppe's son, Giuseppe Antonio (1698–1744), known as *Giuseppe del Gesù* from the *IHS* (*Iesus hominum salvator* or 'Jesus, saviour of mankind') which distinguishes his labels. He sought constantly to improve the violin through experimenting with different materials and designs; as a result, his instruments are held by many to be second only to those of Stradivari.

STRADIVARI

Antonio Stradivari (1644–1737) claimed to have been Nicolo Amati's pupil from 1667 to 1679, although his earliest known instrument is dated 1666. He may have begun as a wood carver under Amati and possibly worked for others in this capacity, since otherwise few instruments survive from these years. His earlier violins reveal Amati's influence and his most highly prized ones date from the first two decades of the 18th century. Several of them are highly ornate, especially in such details as the purfling or tailpiece. The best of these instruments fetch very high prices; Stradivari's cellos and violas, being rarer, higher still. A genuine 'Strad' bears the label *Antonius Stradivarius Cremonensis fecit anno* ('made by Anthony of Cremona in the year'), followed by the year of manufacture. Two of Stradivari's sons, Francesco (1671–1743) and Omobono (1679–1742), were also active as makers under his tutelage.

Renaissance. The strings at this stage were of gut, and would remain so until the 19th century, although a wire-bound *g* string was increasingly common from the start of the 18th. The practice of *scordatura* (that is, tuning the strings to other than their normal pitches) was already known in the 17th century, as witnessed by the *Rosary* sonatas (c.1676) of the Austrian Heinrich Biber.

❉ The Violin in Music

The violin was naturally first used consistently in Italy, but its description as a familiar instrument in Michael Praetorius's *Syntagma musicum* (1618) shows that it must have been established in Germany by this time. Its profile in France was boosted by the establishment in 1626 of Louis XIII's *24 violons du Roi* (actually a string orchestra rather than a collection of violins), which was continued by his successor, Louis XIV, and imitated at the English court of Charles II. It was already accepted practice to divide the violins proper into first and second players; a distinction maintained, with few exceptions, in the modern orchestra. The orchestra would be directed either from the keyboard or by the principal first violin, hence the tradition of regarding this player as the leader of an orchestra. In large-scale 19th- or 20th-century works he or she may be called upon to play major orchestral solos, such as those in Richard Strauss's *Ein Heldenleben* or Rimsky-Korsakov's *Scheherazade*.

The violin's good fortune was to be recognized for its versatility and wide expressive range at a time when instrumental music was in the ascendant. The early Baroque composers had not been slow to employ it in their vocal music, but it was in the expanding field of chamber and later orchestral music that the violin was to achieve a position of dominance, and once again it was Italy which took the lead. Arcangelo Corelli, a gifted violinist himself, developed the three main instrumental forms of the late Baroque. These were the solo sonata for treble instrument and continuo, the trio sonata for two treble instruments and continuo, and the *concerto grosso*. The last-mentioned contrasted a solo group or *concertino*, usually of two violins and cello, with a fuller body, or *ripieno*, of strings and continuo. With the concurrent rise of the solo concerto under composers such as Antonio Vivaldi, the violin emerged as the virtuoso's instrument *par excellence*.

ONE OF LOUIS XIII'S FAMED 'VIOLONS DU ROI', A STRING ORCHESTRA COMPRISING 24 PLAYERS RESIDENT AT THE FRENCH COURT.

Violin Concertos

ANTONIO VIVALDI wrote more than 300 concertos for one or more violins, including the well known 'Four Seasons' which appeared as part of his Op.8 collection *Il cimento dell'armonia e dell'invenzione*.

WOLFGANG AMADEUS MOZART was only seventeen years old when he composed his first violin concerto, in 1773. Two years later, he produced another four, all in the space of six months. The last of them is sometimes called the 'Turkish' Concerto on account of an episode in its rondo which reflects the contemporary fashion for Turkish culture.

LUDWIG VAN BEETHOVEN'S violin concerto is one of the finest works of his middle period and the first of the great 19th-century concertos. When the dedicatee, Clement, complained of its difficulty, the composer is reputed to have replied, "What do I care for your miserable fiddle when I am talking to my God?"

FELIX MENDELSSOHN wrote a concerto for violin and strings while still in his teens, but the work for which he is remembered is the Op. 64 Concerto in E minor (1845). This was written towards the end of his short life, for Ferdinand David, then leader of the Leipzig Gewandhaus orchestra.

JOHANNES BRAHMS wrote his concerto for the famous Hungarian violinist Joseph Joachim. It was for Joachim and the cellist Robert Hausmann that he also wrote the Double Concerto, Op. 102 (1887) – his last orchestral work.

PYOTR IL'YCH TCHAIKOVSKY wrote a concerto for Leopold Auer which the player initially refused to perform on the grounds that it was too difficult. Only after reading a review did the composer become aware that the first performance had been given in Vienna by Adolph Brodsky, to whom he re-dedicated the work in gratitude.

JEAN SIBELIUS, himself a violinist, wrote his only violin concerto in 1903. The version usually heard nowadays is a revision of 1905.

EDWARD ELGAR Many would claim the finest English violin concerto to be that written by Elgar. Completed in 1910, the work was premiered that year by Fritz Kreisler.

ALBAN BERG wrote his hauntingly lyrical violin concerto (1935), originally a commission from the American violinist Louis Krasner, in memory of Alma Mahler's daughter, Manon Gropius, who had died in her teens. The closing pages of the concerto, which was Berg's last completed work, quote the Bach chorale *Es ist genug*.

SERGEI PROKOFIEV'S first violin concerto (Op. 19 in D major) is a youthfully energetic work, composed between 1916 and 1917 when the composer was working on his well known *Classical Symphony*. Its darker-hued companion, Op.63 in G minor, dates from 1935 – the same period as *Peter and the Wolf*.

DMITRI SHOSTAKOVICH, Prokofiev's Russian compatriot, also wrote two violin concertos, both for David Oistrakh. The first was completed in 1948 as Op. 77, but not premiered until 1955 and then in a revised version as Opus 99. The second, one of its composer's last orchestral works (Op. 129), followed in 1967.

ALFRED SCHNITTKE, the contemporary Russian composer, has consistently championed the concerto. The first of his four works in the medium was written in 1957 and revised six years later; the others date from between 1966 and 1984. Schnittke has also written concertos for viola and cello and his six *Concerti grossi* have significant parts for one or more violins.

✄ The Violin and the Bow

The instrument itself was adapted to meet the new demands being made on it. The string player's left hand alters the pitch by stopping the string with the fingers to shorten it. Placing the index finger at differing places on the string is known as 'changing position'. The increasing

PAGANINI, THE MOST CELEBRATED OF ALL VIOLIN VIRTUOSOS AND ONE OF THE MOST ACCOMPLISHED.

use of higher positions led to a lengthening of the neck. The bow, too, changed, losing some of its convexity and becoming standardized in length at around 75cm (30 inches), giving a playing length of some 65cm (26 inches). The bridge would have been flatter than a modern one, facilitating the performance of multiple stops (playing on more than one string at a time), which were now part of the instrument's vocabulary. Composers openly exploited such colouristic devices as *pizzicato*, or plucking the string, and the rapidly reiterated bow-stroke known as *tremolando*. Much of what we know about 18th-century tech-

nique is found in important treatises, such as Leopold Mozart's *Versuch einer gründlichen Violinschule* (1756) or Francesco Geminiani's *The art of playing on the violin* (1751).

A major breakthrough in the development of the modern bow came in the 1780s with a new design by François Tourte. His bow was concave, with an adjustable frog at the heel and a broader hair-width. The hair was prevented from bunching at the frog by means of a ferrule. At the opposite end from the heel, the point assumed its current upward, curving profile to compensate for the maximum concavity at the centre. South American pernambuco was the favoured wood.

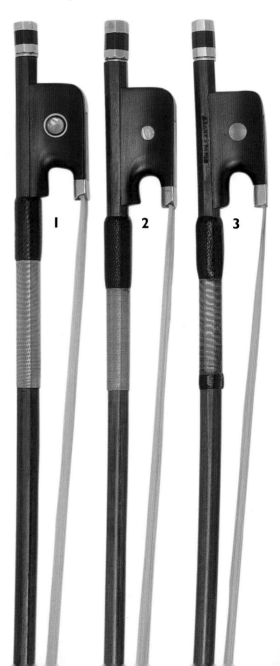

Tourte's design combined lightness – the whole bow weighed around 56 grammes – with power and strength. These innovations played their part in establishing a French school of violin technique equal to that of the hitherto dominant Italians. By the 19th century, and despite the emergence of players like Nicolo Paganini, the Italian school had been virtually overtaken.

♪ BOWS BY FAMOUS MAKERS DISPLAY EXQUISITE CRAFTSMANSHIP AND THE USE OF FINE MATERIALS SUCH AS EBONY, SILVER AND PEARL. BELOW ARE BOWS FOR VIOLIN (1), VIOLA (2) AND CELLO (3–6).

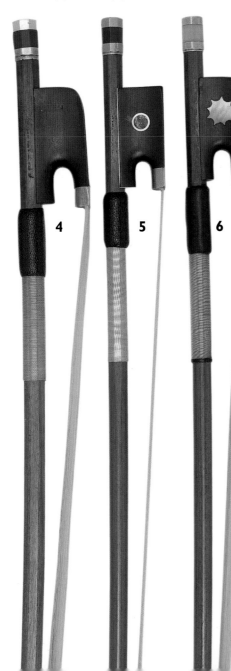

4 5 6

Past Masters

❧

NICOLA MATTEIS was one of the many musicians drawn to the artistic climate of Restoration London, the Neapolitan Matteis is among the earliest recorded violin virtuosos. In London he published a theoretical tutor, *The false consonances of musick* (1682), and four volumes of pieces for violin. Writers including John Evelyn, Roger North and Charles Burney testify to the part he played in introducing the Italian style to England. His son, also called Nicola, taught Burney.

ARCANGELO CORELLI's legacy includes four sets of trio sonatas for two violins and continuo, Op.1–4, the Op.5 solo sonatas and the Op.6 *concerti grossi*. Born in Bologna, he went to Rome in 1671 as a professional violinist. He was the creator of modern violin technique; among his innovations was the exploitation of double and triple-stopping. (Corelli's portrait above right)

FRANCESCO GEMINIANI was a pupil of Corelli who paid his master the compliment of publishing several arrangements of his music. In 1731 he settled in London where he published numerous treatises, of which the most important is *The art of playing on the violin* (1751), credited with being the first comprehensive tutor for the instrument. Geminiani inherited his teacher's interest in technical development and was a pioneer in demanding frequent changes of position.

GIUSEPPE TARTINI was not originally intended for a musical career. He became director of music at the church of St. Antonio in Padua, where he was also active as a violinist and teacher. His interest in acoustics led, in 1714, to his discovery of resultant tones (formed by the difference between two frequencies). Of Tartini's 191 violin sonatas, the most famous is the

so-called *Devil's Trill*. His influential treatise *L'arte dell'arco* contains 50 variations on a gavotte from one of Corelli's Op.5 sonatas.

NICOLO PAGANINI was the last and greatest of the Italian virtuosi; some would say the greatest violinist ever. Of humble Genoese origins, he initially studied the mandolin with his father. He was also an expert guitarist and left many compositions for that instrument as well as for violin. The latter include concertos, chamber music and works for solo violin, all of which testify to his extraordinary technical skill. The last of his 24 *Caprices* for solo violin is the source of the theme used for variations by Rachmaninov, Brahms, Lutoslawski and others.

HENRI VIEUXTEMPS This Belgian-born violinist was a child prodigy who gave his first recital at the age of six. His many violin works include seven concertos, highly thought of in their day, and a number of salon pieces. Vieuxtemps eventually became Professor of Violin at the Brussels Conservatoire, where his pupils included Eugène Ysaÿe.

HENRYK WIENIAWSKI succeeded Vieuxtemps at the Conservatoire. Polish-born, he studied in Paris and toured widely as a virtuoso. He is one of the few composer-virtuosos whose output was not wholly dominated by music for his own instrument.

JOSEPH JOACHIM's compositions may not be as popular now as during his lifetime, but the Hungarian violinist is remembered as a friend of Brahms and the dedicatee of his violin concerto.

PABLO DE SARASATE, a Spanish contemporary of Brahms, wrote a series of *Spanish dances* which retain their popularity as showpieces.

✄ *The Violin as Performer*

The violin of the early 19th century is essentially the instrument as it appears today. The neck is somewhat longer than in the violin of the preceding century, because playing up to the seventh position was now taken for granted. To facilitate this, the angle of the neck was made more pronounced and a sturdier bass-bar and soundpost incorporated to withstand higher

string tension and to give more power to the sound. Many older violins were adapted to accommodate these changes. Strings were still of gut and the *d'* and *a* strings were now sometimes wound with wire as the *g* had been for several decades, although the all-metal *e'* string was still unknown. The bridge supporting the strings was generally more arched. One important addition of the period was the introduction of the chin-rest, an invention attributed to the composer and violin virtuoso, Louis Spohr. This freed the left hand from any role in supporting the instrument

YEHUDI MENUHIN BEGAN HIS CAREER AS A CHILD PRODIGY AND DEVELOPED INTO ONE OF THE WORLD'S MOST RENOWNED PLAYERS.

and allowed for a greater use of *vibrato*, the conscious oscillation in the sound effected by the fingers of the left hand; this had previously been used more sparingly as an expressive device.

Numerous other techniques had become accepted by the 19th century, although used with varying frequency. They include playing *col legno* (that is, with the wood of the bow), first required by Haydn in his Symphony No. 67 (c.1778); and *sul ponticello* (on the bridge), which gives a particularly eerie, nasal sound. Harmonics are produced by touching, rather than pressing, an open or stopped string at specific points. They are a great feature of certain virtuoso showpieces, as is left-hand *pizzicato* used in conjunction with bowed notes. Older recordings also show how much the tradition of sliding between notes, or *portamento*, survived into the early decades of the present century. To these colouristic effects the 20th century has added the so-called 'Bartók pizzicato', where the string is plucked with sufficient force for it to rebound on the fingerboard. Electronic amplification has also been tried, especially where the violin is employed in jazz or folk music.

THE 'DORIA' VIOLIN BY OMOBONO STRADIVARI, YOUNGER SON, AND PUPIL, OF THE RENOWNED CREMONESE MAKER ANTONIO STRADIVARI.

Violin Virtuosos
OF THE 20TH CENTURY

FRITZ KREISLER Many of the great players of the Romantic era were still active when Kreisler was born. He died in an age which deemed technical wizardry alone insufficient qualification for immortality and where recorded sound could broadcast the artistry of the few to an audience of millions. Born in Vienna, where he studied with Hellmesberger and Dont, Kreisler eventually settled in the United States and took US citizenship. Unlike his predecessors, whose chief vehicle for display was their own music, Kreisler was renowned as a great interpreter and advocated re-evaluation of the violin's early repertoire. To this end he even promoted pieces of his own composition, which he ascribed to older masters. His lighter pieces are the staple of the recitalist's encore repertoire. He gave the first performance of the Elgar concerto.

JASCHA HEIFETZ, whom many would put on a par with Kreisler, was born in Vilna, Lithuania. He, too, became an American citizen. Heifetz made his recital debut at the age of five and a year later performed the Mendelssohn Concerto. He was only eleven when he tackled the Tchaikovsky Concerto in public, in Berlin under Artur Nikisch. His technique was flawless and always placed at the service of the music. Among the numerous concertos written for him is that by Walton. He retired from solo playing around 1970, but continued to teach.

JOSEF SZIGETI, a Hungarian and yet another adoptive American, was the co-dedicatee (with the clarinettist Benny Goodman) of Bartók's *Contrasts*. He epitomized the notion that musicianship is ultimately more important than mere technical brilliance.

GINETTE NEVEU would undoubtedly be recognized as one of the finest players of her generation if she had she not died in a plane crash at the age of 30. A child prodigy who studied with Menuhin's teacher, George Enescu, and Carl Flesch, she beat David Oistrakh into second place at the 1935 International Wieniawski Competition. Poulenc dedicated his Sonata to her.

DAVID OISTRAKH went on to become the most famous Russian violinist of the post-war period, premiering major works by, among others, Shostakovich and Prokofiev. His son and most illustrious pupil, Igor Oistrakh, now wears his father's crown.

YEHUDI MENUHIN is honoured as much for his skills as an educationalist and conductor as for his violin playing. Another child prodigy, he made a memorable recording of Elgar's concerto under the composer. The Menuhin School, which he founded in Surrey in 1963, is an important training ground for young musicians. His enquiring mind has led him in the direction of Indian music and, in 1973, he recorded an album with the jazz violinist Stephane Grappelli. Among the many works written for him is Bartók's unaccompanied Sonata.

ISAAC STERN, an American violinist of Russian origin, is a grand-pupil of Adolph Brodsky, having studied with his protégé, Naoum Blinder. Open-minded in his approach to new repertoire, he premiered the Concerto (1985) by Peter Maxwell Davies. A noted chamber musician, he founded a successful piano trio with Eugene Istomin and Leonard Rose in 1961.

ITZHAK PERLMAN, the child of Israeli parents, is equally at home in chamber music as in the concerto repertoire, like his compatriot, Stern. After studying at the Juilliard School he launched a brilliant career with a Carnegie Hall debut in 1963.

𝄞 VIOLA

IT IS IRONIC THAT the instrument regarded for much of its history as the Cinderella of the string family should bear the name from which those of its members are derived. *Viola* is simply the Italian word for 'viol'. Throughout the 16th and early 17th century it is usually found with the designation *da gamba* or *da braccio* to indicate the family of instruments to which it belonged. The viola, like the violin, appears in the Saronno Cathedral frescoes of c.1535. By the end of the 16th century it had established itself as the alto or tenor instrument of the violin family.

𝄞 THIS CLOSE-UP SHOWS THE METICULOUS FINISH ENJOYED BY THE BEST STRINGED INSTRUMENTS. NOTE THE FINE GRAIN AND THE DECORATED EDGE TO THE BODY, KNOWN AS 'PURFLING'.

℁ Construction

The existence of numerous violas from the late Renaissance and early Baroque periods shows that it was frequently made in different sizes, with the smaller instruments used for the higher middle parts in ensemble playing and larger ones for the lower parts. The *c, g, d', a'* tuning, a fifth below the violin, was the same for each. Even today the viola remains the most variable in size of the string family. In order for it to be as acoustically perfect as the violin, it needs to be half as long again, rendering it unplayable on the shoulder. The resultant compromise, giving an instrument of anywhere between 38 and 45 centimetres (15–18 inches) in length, has played its part in the viola's slow emergence as a solo instrument compared with the violin and cello.

℁ In Performance

Nevertheless, the survival of numerous instruments from the 16th and 17th centuries shows that the viola's role as a harmonic filler, if humble, was deemed essential. Five-part string textures, with two violas, are not uncommon in 17th-century French music, for example; Jean-Baptiste Lully for one was especially fond of them. Yet the viola could never compete in brilliance with the violin, nor could it share the cello's usefulness in providing a continuo bass. Viola players, who were rarely, if ever, specialists, were not expected to possess the same level of proficiency as violinists. They were the beginners, the also-rans or, in contemporary parlance, "horn players who had lost their teeth".

Besides, the musical language of the high Baroque was conceived essentially in three parts. The viola had no place in the trio sonata for two treble instruments and continuo, or its orchestral counterpart, the *concerto grosso*'s preferred *concertino* group of two violins and cello. Only at the very end of the period do we find composers, such as Francesco Geminiani, expanding the *concertino* to include a solo viola.

In the orchestral music of the late Baroque and early Classical era the viola, where it was not omitted entirely, was frequently called upon to double the second violins at the unison or, more commonly, the bass line an octave higher. This latter practice died hard, so that even in early 19th century scores such doubling is extremely

THE GERMAN COMPOSER PAUL HINDEMITH, HIMSELF A VIOLA PLAYER OF GREAT DISTINCTION, CONTRIBUTED MAJOR WORKS TO THE INSTRUMENT'S REPERTOIRE, INCLUDING A NUMBER OF SONATAS AND *CONCERTANTE* PIECES WITH ORCHESTRA.

common in orchestral *tuttis*. Composers were, moreover, reluctant to entrust any important thematic material to the violas. For example, as late as his Ninth Symphony (1824) we find Beethoven, in the slow movement, doubling the violas with the second violins as a safety measure. Imagine the surprise, perhaps even shock, experienced by the viola players at the first rehearsals for Tchaikovsky's Symphony No. 6 in B minor, the *Pathétique* (1893), who found themselves expected to play the main theme of the first movement *on their own*.

Viola Concertos

J.S. BACH The viola's long neglect as a solo instrument has left it with only a minimal number of concertos from the Baroque era. By far the most important is Bach's sixth 'Brandenburg' Concerto (c. 1718), a chamber concerto in which the two upper parts are taken by a pair of violas, accompanied by two viole da gamba with cello and bass. The violas and cello alone play in the trio-sonata style slow movement.

GEORG PHILIPP TELEMANN Bach's contemporary was reputedly the most prolific composer in Western music, so it is not surprising that he wrote the first concerto for solo viola to survive in the repertoire. This is the concerto in G major; there is also a concerto for two *violetti*, also in G major.

WOLFGANG AMADEUS MOZART A violist himself, Mozart gave the instrument a prominent role in many of his chamber works but left no solo concerto. What we do have is the magnificent *Sinfonia concertante* (K364) for violin, viola and orchestra, written in 1779. Mozart's intention, rarely observed these days, was that the solo viola should be tuned a semitone higher so as to balance the violin in brilliance; since the work is in E flat, the viola would thus have to play in the brighter key of D major, allowing for more use of open strings. In all three movements the orchestral violas, like the violins, are divided into firsts and seconds. Mozart sketched but never completed a similar work for violin, viola, cello and orchestra.

HECTOR BERLIOZ The two finest *concertante* works from the 19th century are not concertos at all. When Paganini approached Berlioz for a solo work to show

off a Stradivari viola he had acquired, the response was *Harold in Italy*, a symphony with viola *obbligato* which Paganini dismissed as insufficiently virtuosic. Inspired by Byron's *Childe Harold*, this programmatic work of 1834 casts the soloist as the eponymous hero.

RICHARD STRAUSS adopted a similar technique to Berlioz in his tone-poem *Don Quixote* of 1897, personifying Quixote and Sancho Panza as, respectively, solo cello and viola.

WILLIAM WALTON Completed in 1929 and revised in 1961, the concerto by Walton established him as a major young force in English music. Despite being one of the composer's earliest and most lyrical scores, it was rejected as too modern by its intended executant, Lionel Tertis, and the premiere was given by Hindemith.

PAUL HINDEMITH did more than any other composer to enrich the 20th-century repertoire with works for an instrument he played himself. As well as several sonatas for viola, he composed four *concertante* works with orchestra: *Kammermusik No. 5* (1927), *Konzertmusik* (1930), a concerto (*Der Schwanendreher*), based on folk material (1935), and the *Trauermusik* (1936), written at short notice in memory of King George V.

BELA BARTOK The virtuoso player William Primrose commissioned a concerto from Bartók in 1945. Left incomplete at the composer's death, the piece was reconstructed from Bartók's sketches by Tibor Serly and in this form is accepted as a core work in the violist's repertoire.

ABOVE: LIONEL TERTIS, A
GREAT 20TH CENTURY ENGLISH
PIONEER OF THE VIOLA. HE
FAVOURED A LARGE INSTRUMENT.

LEFT: AN ITALIAN VIOLA FROM
THE SCHOOL OF GASPARO DA
SALÒ, C. 1600.

℁ The Viola Comes of Age

Real liberation for the viola came through the medium of chamber music, and most of all through the emergence of the string quartet, yet even here the path to equality was by no means smooth. In several early quartets by Joseph Haydn, the composer who did more than any other to develop the genre, the viola is still to be seen chasing the cello in octaves or at the unison. It is only with the ground-breaking Op. 33 quartets of 1781 that the egalitarian ideal is truly achieved.

A further step forward is taken in the string quintets of Wolfgang Amadeus Mozart. These use two violas, with the first player, along with the violinist, often enjoying a *concertante* role, as in the slow movement of the C major quintet (K515). However, even Mozart's quintets found few immediate imitators and his piano quartets, which added a viola to the more familiar three-some of piano, violin and cello, were regarded as a commercial risk. Ironically, the most familiar Mozart's trios is the so-called *Kegelstadt* ('Skittle-ground') Trio for clarinet, viola and piano (K498), which Mozart is said to have composed while playing skittles.

To play an effective part in chamber music the violist would require more technical facility than his or her orchestral counterpart. Taking a role equal to that of the violin or cello demanded a greater proficiency in the higher positions, for example. By the 19th century this was taken for granted. Violists would have a rewarding time in works such as the youthful Octet of Mendelssohn or the two string sextets by Brahms. Unlike their predecessors, who scorned the viola's lack of brilliance, the Romantic composers valued the viola precisely because of its darker, rather veiled sound, thereby opening up a whole new world of possi-bilities for the orchestral player. At the same time the solo repertoire remained small. There are no major concertos and precious few sonatas, although examples exist by Mendelssohn and Glinka, and Brahms' two sonatas for clarinet pre-scribe the viola as an alternative. The charming *Märchenbilder* of Robert Schumann should not be forgotten, either. Nor were there any important tutors; viola technique was still held to be little different from the violin's.

A change of attitude has finally come about in the present century, principally through the pioneering efforts of players such as Lionel Tertis and William Primrose and of the composer and violist Paul Hindemith. No longer seen as the preserve of second-rate violinists, the viola now enjoys parity with its smaller and larger compan-ions. The result has been a larger solo repertoire than at any other time in its history, and a grow-ing one at that. With this resurgence in the viola's popularity, the instrument preferred by Bach, Mozart and Schubert has finally taken its rightful place on the concert platform.

Famous Violists

THE SPECIALIST VIOLA PLAYER IS A RECENT PHENOMENON, A REFLECTION OF THE INSTRUMENT'S HISTORICAL LACK OF STATUS. MANY PLAYERS OF THE PAST, PARTICULARLY ORCHESTRAL MUSICIANS, WOULD HAVE BEEN PRIMARILY VIOLINISTS. NEVERTHELESS, SEVERAL COMPOSERS OF THE 18TH AND 19TH CENTURIES ARE KNOWN TO HAVE PREFERRED TO PLAY THE VIOLA, NOTABLY J. S. BACH, MOZART AND SCHUBERT. THE FIRST GREAT VIRTUOSO WHOSE NAME IS LINKED WITH THE INSTRUMENT IS ALSO BETTER REMEMBERED AS A VIOLINIST.

NICOLO PAGANINI not only played but wrote for the viola, even though his compo-sitions for it are far less numerous than those for the violin. The most important are a *Terzetto concertante* for viola, cello and guitar (1833) – Paganini was also a noted guitarist – and the intriguingly entitled *Sonata per gran viola* (1834) with orchestra, the 'large viola' of the title being a five-stringed instrument. Paganini's rejection of what would have become the finest work in his viola repertoire is dis-cussed in the feature Viola Concertos on page 17 (see under Berlioz).

LIONEL TERTIS was the pioneer of the viola's rehabilitation as a solo instrument. Initially a violin student at the Leipzig Conservatoire, the English-born Tertis was prompted to devote himself to the viola by his experience in playing quartets. In his long career he toured as a virtuoso and recounted his experiences in three books, *Beauty of tone in string playing* (1938) and two autobiographical works, the appropri-ately named *Cinderella no more* (1953) and *My viola and I* (1974). Tertis was the inspira-tion for several 20th-century viola works, including Walton's Concerto; his main shortcoming as far as the history of the viola is concerned was a lack of sympathy with contemporary music. Only belatedly did he warm to the Walton and he never played any of Hindemith's viola works.

WILLIAM PRIMROSE also began as a vio-linist and took up the viola at the suggestion of his teacher, Ysaÿe. Much of the Scotsman's career was in the United States; he led the violas in Toscanini's NBC Symphony Orchestra from 1937 to 1942 and later taught at the universities of Southern California and Indiana. He founded his own quartet in 1937, published *A method for violin and viola players* in 1960 and is best known for having commissioned Bartók's unfinished concerto.

FREDERICK RIDDLE, at one time principal viola with the London Philharmonic and Royal Philharmonic, was an enthusiastic champion of contemporary music. He made the first recording of Walton's con-certo in 1937 and is the dedicatee of concertos by Martin Dalby and Justin Connolly.

YURI BASHMET is considered by many to be the finest violist of his generation – and certainly the only one to cite playing guitar in a rock band as a formative influence. He switched to viola only in his teens after starting his musical education as a violinist. Thereafter he studied with Vadim Borisovsky at the Moscow Conservatoire. Bashmet won the prestigious Munich Competition in 1976. He is the founder of the Moscow Soloists, with whom he pre-miered Schnittke's Concerto, and has appeared with leading orchestras worldwide.

CELLO

THE FULL NAME of the cello is violoncello, which literally means 'little violone' – the violone being the double bass. Paradoxically, although the cello was fairly quick to achieve a recognizably modern form, its name emerged only in the 17th century, some century or so after the instrument itself. One of its earliest designations was, confusingly, *basso di viola da braccio*, a correct if clumsy attempt to indicate that it was the bass of the family of 'arm viols' – the violins – as opposed to the viols which were held, like the cello, between the knees. In England the simple name bass violin persisted for much of the 17th century, paralleled in France by the equivalent *basse de violon*, although both were eventually to take on a distinct meaning of their own.

℅ Tuning

Once again it is Agricola's *Musica instrumentalis deudsch* which provides us with our first description of the cello, in this case a three-stringed instrument tuned *F, c, g*, giving the instrument the same pitch relationship to the viola as that instrument has to the violin. Consequently, when a fourth string was added, it was the *B flat* below the bottom *F*. Several 16th-century theorists refer to such a tuning, but as early as 1532 the modern tuning *C, G, d, a* is mentioned in Gerle's *Musica teusch*. The second part of Michael Praetorius *Syntagma musicum* (1619) describes both the modern tuning and one a fourth higher (*F, c, g, d*) and illustrates a five-stringed cello, tuned *F', C, G, d, a*. This instrument, which goes almost as low as the modern double bass, was obviously too large to be held between the knees, because it is shown with a tail-pin.

The higher pitched modern tuning certainly appears to have been commoner in Italy by the beginning of the 17th century. The lower tuning seems to have been indicated for the English bass violin and the French *basse de violon*, and this was retained in both countries into the early 18th century.

℅ Fingering and Bowing

Although the cello is tuned in fifths like the violin and viola, its larger size precludes the adoption of their pattern of fingering. In first position on the cello the index finger will give a tone above the open string, but two fingers are

'A MUSIC PARTY' (1733), BY PHILIP MERCIER, SHOWING THE CELLO-PLAYING FREDERICK, PRINCE OF WALES, AND HIS SISTERS.

necessary for a further tone and the fourth finger provides the next semitone or tone. The implications of this for changes of position, coupled with the somewhat more arched left-hand technique which the early cello inherited from the violin, may account for experiments with smaller or five-stringed instruments as a means of extending the compass upwards. Not until the 1720s, when the modern, flatter left-hand position gained ground, did players realize the potential of the left thumb in acting as a bar across the string, like the guitar's *capo dastro*. At the same time the length of the instrument was standardized at around 75cm (30 inches), a development credited to Antonio Stradivari.

Bowing technique also underwent change in the 18th century. Before this time pictures show either an underhand grip, as on the viol, or an overhand one further away from the heel than is common today, limiting movement. Freeing the whole of the bow went hand-in-hand with the developments in fingering technique. The bow itself became more curved as the century progressed. All in all the player gained more control over the bow, with a concomitant potential not just for producing a bigger sound but a broader range of articulation and expression.

The dawn of the 19th century saw a drawing together of the various approaches which had hitherto characterized cello playing. Before Jean-Louis Duport's *Essai sur le doigté du violoncelle et sur la conduite de l'archet* (c.1813) there had been no major tutor and significant variations existed between largely nationalist schools. Thanks to Duport's development of a workable system of fingering, use of the thumb in the higher positions, where the shorter vibrating string allowed for fingering as on the violin, was now taken for granted. So, too, were other techniques pioneered by the violin, such as multiple-stopping

and harmonics. The instrument itself was little changed except in two significant respects. It was no longer gripped between the knees but supported on a tail-pin resting on the floor. As players closer to the present day have shown, the longer the tail-pin, the less vertical the playing position and therefore the greater freedom enjoyed by the left hand. The bow had by this time also acquired the concave profile developed in the late 18th century and was shorter and thicker than that of the violin and viola.

AN ENGLISH CELLO MADE AROUND 1830–40 BY ARTHUR AND JOHN BETTS.

Cello
VIRTUOSOS OF THE PAST

THE DUPORTS Like his Italian contemporary Luigi Boccherini, Jean-Louis Duport served as a cellist to both the Spanish and Prussian courts. Despite writing the first major tutor for the cello and being a brilliant player, he is possibly less well-remembered than his brother Jean-Pierre, also a cellist at the Prussian court, for whom Beethoven intended his Op. 5 sonatas, despite dedicating them to Duport's cello-playing employer, Friedrich Wilhelm II. Both brothers also composed for the instrument. Mozart's visit to the court at Potsdam in 1789 resulted in the three Prussian String Quartets, parts of which give prominence to the cello, and the piano variations, K573, based on a minuet from one of Jean-Pierre's sonatas.

BERNHARD ROMBERG The most famous player of the generation succeeding the Duports was the German Romberg, author of a *Méthode de violoncelle* (1840) and several solo works.

DAVID POPPER The Czech-born Popper gave the classic encore piece *Elfentanz* to the cello repertoire. His Op. 66 of 1892 for three cellos and orchestra is unique in being a Requiem entirely devoid of voices.

Other distinguished cellists of the 19th century include the Italian Alfredo Piatti and the German Julius Klengel, both of whom wrote minor works for their instrument.

✠ In Performance

One obvious result of these developments was the cello's increasing appeal as a solo instrument. Although its solo repertoire in the Baroque period was not negligible, it had been valued more as a useful continuo bass, a role it had fulfilled since the rise of the continuo principle in the early 17th century. By the middle of the 18th century the popularity of the bass viol was also in decline, even in France where it had held its own against the cello for longest. Ironically, the ascendancy of the piano had only a minimal effect in releasing the cello from its assumed place in chamber music. Whereas the keyboard moved from subservience to dominance, the cello often clung to its old role. Mozart's piano trios may occasionally allow the cello to step into the limelight, but Haydn's tie it down to doubling the piano's bass line. Only where the piano was absent, as in the string quartet, was the cello offered a real chance of coming to the fore.

In the orchestra, too, the cello had established itself as the natural bass (as opposed to

𝄢 THE RUSSIAN-BORN CELLIST MSTISLAV ROSTROPOVICH, SEEN HERE REHEARSING WITH BENJAMIN BRITTEN IN 1961.

PABLO CASALS, ONE OF THE CELLO'S
GREATEST CHAMPIONS IN THE 20TH
CENTURY, DID MUCH TO REHABILI-
TATE BACH'S SUITES AS CORE REPERTORY.

contrabass) of the string group which formed its core. Nevertheless, it was a rare composer of the Classical period who treated the orchestral cello section in anything like a soloistic capacity. Solos for the principal player, such as are found in some of Haydn's symphonies (for example, No. 13 of 1763 and No. 95 of 1791) or Zerlina's *Batti, batti* aria in Mozart's *Don Giovanni* are exceptions to a norm. In the opera house, the continuo remained for dry recitative. Beethoven's fourth piano concerto (1806–7) contains a late example of the cello providing a quasi-continuo function in an orchestral work.

The cello now developed two distinct personalities. It could still be called upon to fulfil its traditional function as the bass line in orchestral or chamber music, but expansion of its range released a melodic capacity which the Romantic composers were not slow to exploit. A good

Cello Concertos

BAROQUE

Outside the *concerto grosso*, where the cello provided the bass to the *concertino* group, the composers of the Baroque did not automatically think of the cello as a solo instrument. The first concertos are those by Giuseppe Jaccini, in 1701, and Antonio Vivaldi, who wrote a small number of concertos for one or two cellos as well as six sonatas with continuo. A compatriot of Jaccini and Vivaldi, Leonardo Leo published six concertos in the 1730s.

CLASSICAL

BOCCHERINI Not until the Classical period, with the liberation of the cello from its duty as continuo provider, was the instrument's increasingly important role in chamber music paralleled by an expanded concerto repertoire. Among the earliest Classical concertos of note are those by Luigi Boccherini. One of these, a concerto in B flat major (c. 1770), achieved later popularity in an edition by the cellist Leopold Grützmacher; in this the scoring was expanded, the solo line re-written and the slow movement from a different work substituted.

HAYDN Boccherini's contemporary produced two fine concertos. The one in D major was for a long time ascribed to his pupil Anton Kraft until the reappearance of the manuscript established Haydn's authorship. The C major concerto was known only from an entry in its composer's own catalogue of works until its rediscovery in Prague in 1961. Up to three other cello concertos allegedly by Haydn remain lost.

BEETHOVEN wrote, in addition to five sonatas for cello and piano, the so-called 'Triple Concerto', Op. 56, which calls for a solo group consisting of piano, violin and cello. Completed in 1804, it is one of the most expansive works of his middle period and frequently gives the cello the lion's share of the solo material.

ROMANTIC

SCHUMANN Among the earliest concertos of the Romantic period is Schumann's Op. 129, written in 1850. Like the near-contemporaneous violin concerto by Mendelssohn, this dispenses with the opening orchestral *tutti* of Classical precedent and plays without a break between movements. Schumann uses material freely between movements, even to the extent of beginning the last of the three with a resumé of what has gone before, as in the last movement of Beethoven's Ninth Symphony.

SAINT-SAENS wrote two cello concertos; the second (Op. 119 in D minor), of 1902, remains little known but the first, Op. 33, has always been a favourite with cellists, as has the concerto by his fellow Frenchman, Edouard Lalo.

BRAHMS On the evidence of his chamber music, in which the darker-toned lower strings are often singled out for favourable treatment, Brahms might have written a splendid cello concerto. Instead, we have the Double Concerto, Op. 102, for violin, cello and orchestra. His last orchestral work, written for Joseph Joachim and Robert Hausmann, as in Beethoven's Triple Concerto it affords the cello most opportunities to shine. Brahms also included a long solo for the principal cello in the slow movement of his Second Piano Concerto.

DVORAK arguably wrote the finest 19th-century concerto. Brahms is alleged to have said that, had he known it was possible to write such a work, he would have done so. The B minor Concerto, Op. 104, is actually Dvořák's second; an early essay in A major, dating from 1865, survives in piano score. A late work, Op. 104 was begun in 1894, while the composer was in the United States, and finished the following year in Prague. Dvořák intended it for the Czech cellist Hanuš Wihan, but the first performance was given by Leo Stern in London in 1896.

example of the coexistence of both elements can be seen in a work such as Schubert's late String Quintet with two cellos. The second cello can maintain the bass of the ensemble, leaving the first to soar into its high register. The two Sextets by Brahms also revel in this duality. In the orchestral repertoire the 19th century yields such celebrated passages as the opening of Rossini's *William Tell* overture (with five solo parts), the overture to Glinka's *Ruslan and Lyudmila*, the third movement of Brahms' Third Symphony and the Offertorium of Verdi's *Requiem*. From there it was but a short step to composers expecting orchestral cellists to cope easily with passages like the opening of Stravinsky's *Petrushka* or the slow movement of Elgar's First Symphony.

LUIGI BOCCHERINI. HIS CONCERTOS ARE AMONG THE EARLIEST STILL TO HAVE A REGULAR PLACE IN THE CELLO REPERTOIRE.

Chamber Works

❧

BAROQUE TO ROMANTIC

BACH The six suites for solo cello by J. S. Bach are important, not just as the first works we have for unaccompanied cello but as the first significant contribution to the repertoire by a non-cellist. Their chief glory lies in the skill with which Bach's melodic lines suggest a rich harmonic texture. They date from the 1720s when Bach was Kapellmeister at Cöthen and may have been intended for the court cellist Christian Linike. The fifth suite uses *scordatura*. The sixth was written for viola pomposa; see under Violino Piccolo, page 44.

Sonatas with continuo become more numerous towards the end of the Baroque period and survive in those written later by Boccherini.

BEETHOVEN Otherwise the emergent duo sonata of the Classical era rarely favoured the cello. This has left the Op. 5 sonatas (1796) of Beethoven in a pioneering position. They were commissioned by Friedrich Wilhelm II of Prussia. Beethoven produced three more sonatas; the isolated Op. 69 in A major (1808) and the two sonatas Op. 102 (1815), in C major and D major, which stand at the threshold of his final period.

MENDELSSOHN's two sonatas are often overlooked. The first, Op. 45 (1838), was written, like the earlier *Variations concertantes* (1829), for the composer's brother, Paul. The second, Op. 58 (1843), is a splendid work which was praised by Schumann; it was intended for the Polish Count Mateusz Wielhorski, a pupil of Romberg.

SCHUMANN himself composed a set of *Five pieces in folk style* for cello and piano and sanctioned the use of the cello in the Op. 70 *Adagio and allegro* and the Op. 73 *Fantasiestücke*, intended for horn and clarinet respectively. All were composed in 1849.

CHOPIN and **RACHMANINOV** were pianist/composers whose rare forays into the field of chamber music yielded a sonata for cello and piano apiece.

BRAHMS More frequently heard are the two sonatas by Brahms, Op. 38 in E minor (1865) and Op. 99 in F major (1886).

There is also a sonata, Op. 6 in F major, by the young Richard Strauss (1883), and two sonatas by Fauré (1917 and 1921).

MODERN CHAMBER REPERTOIRE
Many composers have enriched the cello's chamber repertoire in the 20th-century.

The Hungarian Zoltan Kodály's contribution includes an unaccompanied sonata (1915), a sonata with piano (1909–10) and a *Duo* for violin and cello (1914). The last genre was also represented by Ravel in his Sonata (1920–2). The Czech Martinů produced three sonatas and two sets of variations with piano. Shostakovich and Prokofiev each wrote a single sonata with piano and there is a fine one by their compatriot, Schnittke. Benjamin Britten wrote a sonata with piano and three solo suites for Mstislav Rostropovich.

Unaccompanied works, exploiting the cello's wide range and expressive potential, have proliferated in the post-war period. In addition to the Britten suites can be cited the *Serenade* by Henze, the Sonata by the American George Crumb and the *Trois strophes sur le nom de Sacher* by Henri Dutilleux, one of many such works commissioned for the conductor Paul Sacher's seventieth birthday in 1976 and based on his name. The biennial Manchester Cello Festival has become established as a showcase for the performance of new works and attracts the participation of leading players from all over the world.

JACQUELINE DU PRE WAS FAMED FOR HER ELECTRIFYING PERFORMANCES. SHE IS SEEN HERE IN CONCERT WITH HER HUSBAND DANIEL BARENBOIM.

℅ Versatility and Virtuosity

For the various virtuosos produced by the 19th century, technical brilliance could often become an end in itself. As with the violin, emphasis in the present century has shifted towards exploration and interpretation of a wider repertoire. The remarkably high number of first-rate cellists which the 20th century has produced, and continues to produce, testifies to the versatility which is today one of the instrument's most prized assets. There are now probably more major 20th-century works for solo cello than for solo violin. The 20th century has produced several concertos

of the first rank, not least that by Edward Elgar, a late work (1919), full of autumnal beauty and post-war melancholy. Dmitri Shostakovich wrote two concertos; the first, Op. 107 (1959), has to date proved more popular than its successor, Op. 126, of 1966. The Polish composers Krzystof Penderecki and Witold Lutoslawski have both written concertos, the latter's being one of the best from recent decades.

At the same time it has become apparent that our knowledge of the cello's early repertoire is far from exhaustive. Fortunately, there are now a number of makers producing excellent copies of 17th- and 18th-century orchestral stringed instruments. 𝄡

Cello Virtuosos
OF THE MODERN ERA
℅

No-one did more than Pablo Casals to promote the cello in the 20th century. His career was already established by 1900, partly due to support from the Spanish royal family. He died in 1973, aged 97. One of the many debts owed to him is for the rehabilitation of the Bach suites as core repertoire. Casals was also a composer of some ability, and not merely for his instrument. His first wife was Klengel's pupil, Guilhermina Suggia.

Great cellists from the mid-century include Gregor Piatigorsky, the Russian who inspired works by Martinů and Hindemith; the Frenchman Pierre Fournier, for whom Albert Roussel and Frank Martin wrote concertos; and his compatriot Paul Tortelier, whose art is distilled in his book *How I play, how I teach* (1975). Among their successors the leading name is that of the Russian Mstislav Rostropovich, dedicatee of Shostakovich's two concertos and Britten's Cello Symphony, Sonata and three suites. The career of the late Jacqueline du Pré was cut short by multiple sclerosis, but she remained a valued teacher and her incandescent playing on record has provided inspiration to many.

From the many outstanding players of the present generation mention should be made of the Americans Ralph Kirshbaum, Lynn Harrell and Yo Yo Ma, the Englishmen Steven Isserlis and Raphael Wallfisch, the Armenian Karine Georgian and the Scandinavians Frans Helmerson and Truls Mørk.

DOUBLE BASS

OF ALL THE MEMBERS of the modern string family the double bass is the only one which can claim real kinship with the viols (see pages 6–7). It is a direct descendant of the *violone* – the 'big viol', which played at 16-foot pitch (that is, sounding an octave lower than written) and which, unlike the smaller viols, succeeded in finding a place in the modern orchestra.

References to double bass viols exist from the early 16th century, and some instruments themselves have survived from only slightly later. Generally with six strings, they display a variety of shapes and tunings, and may or may not have the viols' characteristic fretted neck. The neck itself appears to have been more vertical at this stage and the bridge positioned lower down the belly. Contemporary iconography shows an underhand bow grip.

Six-stringed *violoni* continued to be used throughout the 17th century, taking their place alongside a five-stringed model which was commoner in the German-speaking countries. Such instruments were obviously familiar to several theorists of the following century. Leopold Mozart, in his *Versuch einer gründlichen Violinschule*, criticized the weakness of the sound resulting from the thinness of the strings and noted the danger of hitting the wrong string by mistake, but remarked that "on such a bass one can play difficult passages more easily, and I have heard concerti, trios, solos and such like performed on one of these with great beauty". Johann Albrechtsberger's *Gründliche Anweisung zur Compositionen* (1790) refers to an instrument tuned *F', A', D, F sharp, B* which was fretted, and Joseph Quantz's seminal *Versuch einer Anweisung die Flöte traversiere zu spielen* (1752) supports the retention of frets but prefers the more modern three- or four-string basses which lacked them. Both instruments lived quite happily alongside each other in early 18th-century Germany and Austria, the four-stringed model sometimes tuned in fifths an octave below the cello. This was favoured in France as well. Common tunings for the three-stringed instrument were *G', D, G,* or *A', D, G,* but huge variations still occurred.

Although the fretted *violone* was still around at the beginning of the 19th century, its place in the orchestra had now been taken by its unfretted counterpart. It is in the orchestra that we must trace the instrument's development, since solo repertoire is virtually non-existent before the mid-18th century. Even after the establishment of the string family as the core of the orchestra, instruments of 16-foot pitch could not always be taken for granted. They were unknown in England, for instance, until the 1690s. One of the earliest tutors, Michel Corrette's *Méthodes pour apprendre à jouer de la Contre-basse à 3, à 4 et à 5 cordes* (1773) mentions that a lot of the time, the basses, where they were present, "unfortunately stayed silent".

✶ *The Double Bass Finds its Voice*

The double bass was rarely treated as an independent voice until well into the 19th century. Four-part harmony was complete in the string group of two violins, viola and cello, a distribution which the rise of the string quartet served only to reinforce. The double bass, when it was used, invariably doubled the cello's bass line at the lower octave. This practice, moreover, took little heed of whether the instrument was tuned

THE MODERN DOUBLE BASS RETAINS THE SLOPING SHOULDERS OF THE *VIOLONE* OR DOUBLE BASS VIOL.

Soloist
℘

From Haydn to Peter Maxwell Davies, more composers have taken the double bass seriously as a solo instrument than is popularly imagined. It is a pity that no concerto by Joseph Haydn has survived, but we do have the solos in the trios of his symphonies Nos. 6–8, *Le matin* (c. 1761), *Le midi* (1761), and *Le soir* (c. 1761), and the variation finales of symphonies Nos. 31 (1765) and 72 (1763). Mozart included a bass *obbligato* in his concert aria *Per questa bella mano*, K612 and there exist concertos by his contemporaries Karl Ditters von Dittersdorf, Johann Baptist Vanhal and Giovanni Battista Cimadoro.

Solos within the orchestral repertoire often exploit the bass's capacity for grotesqueness. A famous example is 'The Elephant' in Saint-Saëns' *Carnival of the Animals* (1886). Others feature in the First Symphony (1886) of Gustav Mahler and the ballet *Pulcinella* (1920) by Stravinsky. The solo in Prokofiev's *Lieutenant Kijé* (1934) shows the bass in lyrical rather than comic mode.

♪ A MEDIEVAL WOODCUT SHOWING A GROUP OF DOUBLE BASSISTS. THESE EARLY INSTRUMENTS OFTEN HAD ONLY THREE STRINGS.

in such a way as to make this genuinely achievable. In the Classical and early Romantic periods some concessions were made in that composers might indicate where the basses were to drop out altogether or provide simplified parts where the bass line was deemed too challenging for them to play the notes as written. Not until the 19th century discovered the melodic potential of the cello was the double bass allowed to provide the true bass to the orchestral strings. Even then it was common for composers to show caution and

retain some cellos to play along with the basses. Berlioz was one who advocated this compromise, but then it was usual for French orchestras of the period to have far more cellos than basses, whereas in some countries, notably Italy, the basses often outnumbered the cellos.

Meanwhile, the instrument did enjoy some measure of independence in certain types of chamber music. Before the general availability of the contrabassoon, for example, it could be called upon to add weight to the bass in wind ensembles. Mozart's *Serenade for 13 wind instruments* (K361) is really misnamed, since the *Contra Basso* is clearly marked *pizzicato* at one point. Mozart also wrote several *divertimenti* for 2 horns, 2 violins, viola and *basso*, including the well-known *Musical joke* (1787). The illustration in

SOME NOTABLE
Double Bassists

%

DOMENICO DRAGONETTI A good deal of the bass's concert solo repertoire is the product of composers who were players themselves. In the 19th century two names stand out. One was the Italian Dragonetti, hailed as the 'Paganini of the double bass'. He was born in Venice in 1763 but settled eventually in London, where he was still appearing in public in the 1840s. His concertos, written for a three-stringed instrument, are fiendishly difficult even by modern standards.

GIOVANNI BOTTESINI The second great name is that of Bottesini, a native of Crema and a graduate of the Milan Conservatoire. He travelled extensively as a virtuoso in Europe, Russia and the United States and at Verdi's request conducted the premiere of *Aida* in Cairo in 1871. Bottesini was a prolific composer, writing operas, symphonies and chamber music as well as several concertos and show pieces for his own instrument. As a teacher he published, in the 1860s, a *Metodo completo per contrabbasso*, one of the first tutors seriously to discuss the instrument's solo and orchestral repertoire.

SERGE KOUSSEVITZKY is best remembered as a conductor of the Boston Symphony Orchestra, but he studied the double bass at the Moscow Conservatoire and during his early career as a soloist was known as 'the Russian Bottesini'. He wrote several works for bass, of which the most substantial is the Op. 3 Concerto, first performed by him in 1905.

Other players who have done much to promote the instrument include the Englishmen Eugene Cruft, Rodney Slatford and Duncan McTier (dedicatee of a concerto by Peter Maxwell Davies).

the first edition of that work, plus the analogous example of the solo group in his *Serenata notturna* (1776), indicates that *basso* here means just the double bass and not the usual cello *and* bass. The double bass also features in various works for mixed ensemble by Haydn. Important works from the next generation to call for the double bass include Beethoven's Septet (1800) and Schubert's Octet (1823) and Trout Quintet (1819). As late as Dvořák's Op. 77 Quintet of 1875, the inclusion of the double bass in chamber music for strings alone was still a rarity.

✼ The Modern Instrument

The modern double bass retains the viol's preference for tuning in fourths, rather than fifths. This is to some extent necessitated by the large span required of the left hand. The four strings are now tuned *E', A', D, G*. Modern instruments often have a fifth string tuned to *C'* or *B'*. The low *C'* has been taken for granted by many composers from the turn of the century onwards, and an extra string has proved more satisfactory than simply tuning the *e* string down. For solo work it has been common since the late 18th century to tune the strings up a tone, making the bass a transposing instrument twice over. Conventional parts are written an octave higher than they sound, solo parts a ninth higher. Early double basses were tuned by means of wooden pegs, like the rest of the violin family. These were replaced in the 17th century by wooden cogs; these days the cogs are of metal.

Even today the design of instruments can differ quite significantly, and there is a marked

𝄞 FAR LEFT: A LINE-UP OF DOUBLE BASSES IN A MODERN SYMPHONY ORCHESTRA.

variation in size, with the largest instruments standing nearly a metre and a half tall (5 feet) and the smallest 25–30cm (10–12 inches) or so less. Most instruments have the viol's flat back. This is usual in instruments which keep the characteristic sloping-shouldered shape of the viol, but can also be found in those basses which resemble a large violin. Some schools of playing retain the underhand bowing technique as well.

The publication of Franz Simandl's *Neueste Methode des Contrabass-Spiels* (1874) had been a milestone in the development of bass playing. From the late Romantic period onwards composers felt no compunction in expecting as much from the

𝄞 A DOUBLE BASS OF AROUND 1840. BY THIS TIME IN THE INSTRUMENT'S EVOLUTION, THE FOUR-STRING MODEL HAD BECOME COMMON.

THE DOUBLE BASS IN *Jazz* ✼

The double bass was often used as a 16-foot instrument in the 18th-century wind band. In our own time it is an established member of the wind orchestra and jazz band. A typical 17-piece jazz band of the 1930s or 1940s would contain, in addition to saxes, trumpets and trombones, piano, guitar, bass and drums. Nowadays the bass is invariably played *pizzicato*, sometimes employing *slap* technique, where the string is allowed to bounce off the fingerboard. It has also moved from being a purely rhythmic instrument to a jazz soloist in its own right.

Earlier jazz bassists include John Lindsay and 'Pops' Foster (real name George Murphy Foster), both of whom played in Louis Armstrong's band in the 1930s. Walter Page and Charles Mingus are prominent names from the 1940s. More recently, Ron Carter has successfully used a smaller piccolo bass and published a tutor in jazz playing.

The American Gary Karr, who was born into a family of bass players, has successfully bridged the gap between the worlds of classical music and jazz. As an orchestral player he has appeared with many world-class ensembles, and his interest in expanding the bass's contemporary repertoire has led him to commission several compositions.

bottom end of the string section as from the rest of it. One result has been a latter-day preference for the sloping-shouldered design, which facilitates playing in the higher positions. Players of our own day have shown the double bass to be as versatile an instrument as its smaller brethren, not least in the one area where their presence is minimal – jazz. 𝄡

 HARP

THE HARP IS ONE of the oldest musical instruments we possess. "David took an harp, and played with his hand: so Saul was refreshed" the first book of Samuel tells us, in one of the many biblical references to the instrument. There is every reason to suppose that even then it was an established instrument. In what must be one of the oldest pictorial representations of any instrument, a fragment of Mesopotamian pottery from around 3300 BC shows the harp in its earliest known form. A piece of wood is carved into an arc, between the ends of which are stretched strings of differing lengths giving different pitches. Its origins are likely to be the hunter's bow, whose single, tensed string would resonate at a recognizable pitch when plucked; the shorter the string, the higher the pitch. The addition of some means of amplifying the resonance was all that was needed to turn an everyday weapon into a true musical instrument.

℁ *Angle Harp*

Arch harps such as this are also known from Egyptian paintings of the 3rd century BC. The first actual instrument to survive, also Egyptian, dates from around a thousand years later. The Louvre in Paris possesses a so-called angle harp or *trigonon*. Standing just over 1.05 metres (40 inches) high, it has 21 strings stretched at an angle between a vertical neck which is itself

attached to a horizontal soundboard. Pictorial evidence suggests that such instruments were also common in Greece; indeed, its name is merely the Greek word for 'triangle'. Plato alludes to it in his *Republic*, claiming it inferior to the lyre, or *kithara* , which had fewer strings. There also existed by then a type of angle harp in which the vertical member forms the soundboard with the strings strung from a horizontal pegboard.

℁ *Frame Harp*

During the last centuries BC and the early Christian era, various sizes of arch and angle harp spread first to eastern Asia and later to northern Europe. An important step forward was marked by the emergence of the frame harp. This was an angle harp in which the third side of the

𝄞 TOP: AN EARLY REPRESENTATION, REPUTED TO BE KING DAVID, PLAYING A SIMPLE BOW HARP.

𝄞 LEFT: A CELTIC HARP (IRISH *CLÁIRSEACH*, MEANING 'LITTLE FLAT THING' ALTHOUGH, PERVERSELY, IT WAS BIG AND VERTICAL), WHOSE BASS STRINGS AND HEAVY BODY PRODUCED A STRONG TONE WHEN PLUCKED.

decachordum. From this period also come the first English occurrences of the word 'harp'. The Anglo-Saxon *hearpen*, meaning to play a string instrument, is derived from the Nordic *harpa*.

Although actual instruments from this period are rare, a fairly clear picture emerges of the early medieval European harp as a small, framed instrument with few strings. That this remained a standard design is corroborated by those instruments which have come down to us from the later Middle Ages. The soundboard, with or without soundholes, is towards the player, opposite a (usually curved) forepillar. The strings may have been of metal, perhaps of brass as on the Irish harp, and would have been plucked with the fingernails. The Irish harp itself was larger, with a soundboard made in one piece and between 30 and 36 strings. A famous example from the 14th century, now the Irish national symbol, survives without its strings in Trinity College, Dublin.

By the 16th century the European harp had grown larger than its medieval prototype but remained a diatonic instrument. Its two dozen or so strings, by now often of gut, were tuned to specific notes, making chromatic alteration impossible. Martin Agricola, for example, in his *Musica instrumentalis deudsch* (1529), refers to a three and a half octave instrument, *F* to *c'''*, where the relevant strings could be tuned to *b sharp* or *b flat* as necessary.

✄ Double and Triple Harps

A solution was sought in the double harp. This had a second row of strings tuned in such a way as to provide those notes lacking in the first row. The Italian theorist Vincenzo Galilei describes such a harp, with 58 strings, in his *Dialogo della musica antica e della moderna* (1581). This is the *arpa doppia* scored for in Monteverdi's *Orfeo* (1607). Praetorius illustrates one in the second

AN EGYPTIAN WALL PAINTING OF C. 1500 BC, SHOWING (FROM LEFT) ANGLE HARP, LONG LUTE AND LYRE.

triangle was closed, so that all the strings were enclosed in a wooden frame of which one side acted as a resonator. (This enclosing side is usually referred to as a forepillar.) The modern harp is a frame harp, but the earliest evidence of such instruments, which are depicted in Europe from about the 8th century, shows that they were nothing like the size of their later counterparts. Illuminated manuscripts show a portable instrument, often with ten or sometimes twelve strings. Appropriately enough, many such illustrations are found in psalters, since King David was the alleged author of the psalms. The ten-string instrument he is frequently shown with may represent an attempt to show the Jewish

part of his *Syntagma musicum* (1619), together with a triple harp. This had three rows of strings; the outer ones have an identical tuning, while between them runs a row tuned to those chromatic notes otherwise missing from them. The triple harp was known in England by the middle of the 17th century and proved even more popular in Wales, where it became the standard instrument for virtuosos until well into the 19th century and was often referred to simply as the Welsh harp. This is the instrument associated with the tradition of *penillion*, where a melody is improvised as a counterpoint to an existing one played on the harp. Several fine Welsh-made triple harps survive from the 18th and 19th centuries.

℅ *Pedal Harp*

Attempts at improvement were made as early as the 17th century. Some German single harps of this period have hooks placed at the neck end of certain strings which, when turned by the fingers, raise the pitch by a semitone. This had the double disadvantage of being manually controlled and applicable to only one string at a time. A major breakthrough came with the development of pedal-operated mechanisms to alter the pitch. The first such pedal harp is usually attributed to the Bavarian Jakob Hochbrucker around 1720 (some sources say earlier). Bavaria might have become the European centre for harp making had its thunder not been stolen by Paris, allegedly spurred on by the fact that Marie-Antoinette, like a good many aristocratic women, was a harpist.

A typical French pedal harp of the later 18th century had around 40 strings. The pedal

THIS BEAUTIFULLY CRAFTED 18TH-CENTURY FRENCH HARP BELONGED TO LOUIS XVI'S QUEEN, MARIE-ANTOINETTE.

brought into play a hook, or crochet, which pressed the string against a fixed point, thereby sharpening it. This system was improved by the family firm of Cousineau, who replaced the hook with a pair of levers which turned in opposite directions, gripping the string in the process. The pedals could either be set beforehand to give a basic tuning most amenable to the key of a piece or changed during its course. Sébastien Erard's revolutionary patent harp of 1792 refined this by substituting for the levers two brass forks mounted on a small movable wheel. The pedal action turns the wheel, again in opposite directions, so that the string is gripped by the forks.

All of these systems raise the pitch of a string by half a tone. Cousineau experimented with a second set of pedals which extended the harp's tonal possibilities, albeit in a cumbersome way. But it was Erard, again, who developed the double-action harp which is essentially the instrument of today. His instrument, patented in 1810, tuned its 43 open strings to a scale of *C flat*, with a range of *F flat'* to *f flat''''*. It used the same fork system as his single-action harp. The seven pedals could each be used in two positions, raising the pitch by a half or whole tone respectively. Erard's nephew, Pierre, extended the number of strings to 46, as in the modern concert instrument. Further improvements were made around the turn of the 20th century by the American firm of Lyon-Healy, mainly by enclosing the mechanism (which had been on the outside of the neck in the Erard model) within the neck.

The double harp, in particular, held its own throughout the 19th century and was still favoured in some circles in the early 20th century. Its effective swansong is Debussy's *Danse sacrée et danse profane*, commissioned by the firm of Pleyel in 1904 to show off its double harp. Not to be outdone, the firm of Erard responded by commissioning Ravel's *Introduction et Allegro* (1905) to show off its pedal harp.

MATERIALS USED IN THE MAKING OF

Harps

※

It is likely that various materials were used to make early harps. Irish harps were often strung with brass. Willow was used for their soundboard. English harps before the Norman Conquest of 1066 had strings of twisted horsehair. By the 16th century, these were usually made of gut.

The soundboard of Erard's patent harp of 1792 was made of pine. The neck was made separately of laminated wood and the metal parts of brass. Gut was still used for most of the strings, with the lowest ones of silk wound with wire. Modern developments of this design include the replacement of silk with steel for the lower strings and the strengthening of the soundboard with a layer of veneer.

THE HARP MADE ITS FIRST APPEARANCE IN A SYMPHONY IN 1830. MANY LARGE WORKS FOR ORCHESTRA REQUIRE MORE THAN ONE HARP.

※ *The Harp in the Orchestra*

The harp's appearances in the orchestra were few in the 18th century and restricted to providing special effects. Handel used the instrument, appropriately, in the oratorio *Saul* (1738) and both Gluck and Haydn call for it in their operas on the Orpheus legend – *Orfeo ed Euridice* (1762) and *L'anima del filosofo* (1791) respectively. Elsewhere Handel scored for the harp in a small number of operas and as an alternative to the organ in the concerto Op. 4 No. 6 (1736). Mozart used it once, in his Concerto for flute and harp, K299, as did Beethoven in his ballet music for *Die Geschöpfe des Prometheus* (1801). Bach's son Carl Philipp Emanuel wrote a sonata, and minor pieces were produced by such composers as Johann-Baptiste Krumpholtz, himself a harpist, Mozart's friend Jan Ladislav Dušek, who was married to one, and François Boieldieu. The first appearance of the harp in a symphony is in Berlioz's *Symphonie fantastique* (1830) where, as if to make up for lost time, Berlioz asks for six instruments – but writes only two parts. 𝄢

♪ GUITAR

THE GUITAR HAS a venerable ancestry and can claim to be one of the few stringed instruments to have bridged the divide between classical and popular music with any great success. Yet the fact that it has rarely been used as an orchestral instrument has led many to underestimate its importance and the size of the solo repertoire which it commands.

❧ Origins

The very early history of the guitar remains to some extent unclear. If the distinguishing feature of the instrument is taken to be the manner in which it is held, then plucked instruments of the guitar type, as opposed to harps, existed in the pre-Christian era. A Babylonian clay relief of around 1900 BC shows various instruments which appear to have two or more strings. All have the typical neck of the guitar family and are plucked with the right hand. A Hittite carving of some six hundred years later appears to have a neck with an early form of frets. An actual instrument found in an Egyptian grave of c.1500 BC has a rounded body, rather like the resonators of contemporary harps, but a perfectly straight, elongated neck. Similar instruments were in use in Egypt until the early centuries AD. One important survival, found in a Coptic tomb and now in the Oriental Institute in Heidelberg, is dated to between 400 and 600 AD. It has a flat back and a resonator made in two distinct pieces connected by a ribbed section to form a hollow box with inward curving sides – in short the prototype of the modern guitar.

If, as some authorities claim, such instruments were introduced into Europe by invading Arabs, then we have strong grounds for associating the guitar with the European country where Arab influence was strongest – Spain. The first identifiable depiction of a guitar to come from that country is in an illustrated commentary on the New Testament *Book of Revelations* known to have originated in the monastery of San Miguel de Escalada near Leon in the year 926. One illustration shows four individuals playing long, plucked instruments held either upright or across the knee. Each of these instruments has a pear-shaped body and a neck which diminishes towards a large scroll containing tuning pegs. Although one of them is being played with a bow, the remaining three are being plucked, one with a plectrum. Another illustration from the same source shows a larger number of people with plucked instruments which this time are held across the body and have narrower, parallel necks and three strings. Again, some of the instruments appear to be being played with plectra.

However, this should not be taken as conclusive evidence that the guitar came to Europe via Spain. A German psalter from the same period, for instance, depicts a different kind of instrument, held in most cases almost at right-angles to the player, with an almost square body and parallel neck ending in a disc-shaped scroll into which are inserted tuning pegs. The fact that representations of similar instruments are found in both manuscript and sculptural sources well into the Middle Ages would argue for the existence of an indigenous European tradition co-existing with an imported one.

Another theory postulates that the guitar might have entered Europe via southern France, because Provence was the centre for the medieval troubadour tradition which spread to a number

♪ THE ENTRY OF THE GUITARISTS AT THE GRAND BAL DE LA DOUAIRIERE DE BILLEBAHAUT GIVEN IN 1629.

of other countries, Spain included. Some of the most important evidence is to be found in the highly developed examples of figurative sculpture adorning the large churches of the early Gothic period in England and France – such as the angelic musicians in the Angel Choir at Lincoln Cathedral, the magnificent series in Beverley Minster or at the cathedrals of Chartres and Rheims.

❧ Construction and Tuning

As with the harp, the dawn of the Renaissance marks an important watershed in that from this period onwards we have examples of the instruments themselves to set beside documentary or illustrative evidence. One feature of the contemporary instrument is that its strings were commonly arranged in courses: pairs of strings tuned either to the same pitch or in octaves. Six-course guitars are known from the 15th century.

This arrangement, with the courses tuned in unison, is a feature of the Spanish *vihuela*, a flat-backed plucked instrument popular in the later 15th and 16th centuries. With its barely waisted body and narrow neck it proclaims a link with the proto-guitars of the Middle Ages. Guitars of the 16th century usually had four or five courses and were smaller than their modern counterparts. Tuning might vary, but appears to have displayed a consistent preference for a third between the middle courses and a fourth between them and the highest and lowest ones. The model here is obviously contemporary viol tuning. This pattern of fourths with an interpolated third is reflected in the tuning of the single strings of the modern guitar: *E, A, D, g, b, e'.*

It seems that, while the five-course guitar was preferred as an accompanying instrument, the four-course variety was deemed, like the lute, more suited to polyphonic music. This is confirmed by the first music to be printed for it, in the *Tres libros de musica en cifras para vihuela* prepared in 1546 by the Spaniard Alonso Mudarra. The music is written in tablature, giving, not the

actual notes to be played, but a system of symbols indicating the position of the fingers on each string with symbols indicative of note lengths. Such music would be played, in the terminology still in use, not *rasgueado* (strummed) but *punteado* (plucked). Thus it presupposes the plucking of the strings with the fingers themselves, as in the case of the lute, rather than with a plectrum. Mudarra's publication was followed by a number of others, not least in France where the guitar became enormously popular. The first English tutor, James Rowbotham's *The breffe and plaine instruction for to learne the gitterne*, is a translation of a French publication of 1551. It is unfortunately lost.

In addition to being smaller than the modern guitar, the instrument for which such publications were intended would have had a less pronounced waist (although more pronounced than that of the *vihuela*) and often an intricately carved rose in place of the latter day open soundhole. The back would have been flat. A rounded back is commoner in the five-course instrument known as the *chitarra battente*, used, as mentioned

Guitar Virtuosos

✄

NICOLO PAGANINI played the guitar as well as the violin and left a substantial amount of music for it, including pieces for guitar and violin duo.

FERNANDO SOR, Paganini's Spanish contemporary, was a native of Barcelona who spent the later part of his life mostly in Paris. Encouraged by several composers, he was able to establish himself as a virtuoso guitarist as well as a minor composer of stage works. His large output for the guitar includes a *Méthode pour la guitare*, published in Paris in 1830.

NAPOLEON COSTE had earned a reputation as the finest French guitarist of his time and a worthy rival to Sor (whose *Méthode* he re-edited) by the time an accident ended his playing career in 1863. Coste left numerous guitar works, some of them intended for the large, lower-pitch instrument he favoured. The guitar was the main instrument of Coste's countryman, Hector Berlioz, although he never composed for it.

FRANCISCO TARREGA was the first Spanish guitarist to exploit the innovations of Antonio de Torres Jurado. As important as his own small-scale compositions are the many transcriptions he made of music by other composers, some of which remain in the recitalist's repertoire.

AGUSTIN BARRIOS MANGORE, a Paraguayan, was the first significant Latin American guitarist. A cultured man, he was acutely conscious of the guitar's European roots and the debt it owed to players like Sor. Many of his compositions remain unpublished, but the excellence of his technique has been captured in a number of recordings.

ANDRES SEGOVIA is for many synonymous with the guitar. This remarkable Spanish musician gave his first recital at the age of 14 and was still appearing in public in his eighties. No one did more than he to establish the guitar as a concert instrument, through playing, composing, editing and commissioning music for it. Composers who dedicated works to him include Turina, Roussel, Ponce, Castelnuovo-Tedesco and, most notably, Rodrigo.

DJANGO REINHARDT, the Belgian jazz guitarist, was forced to develop a technique using only two fingers after damaging his left hand in a fire in 1928. In the 1930s he was a founder, with the violinist Stephane Grappelli, of the celebrated Quintette du Hot Club de France. He later worked with Duke Ellington. His playing had a profound influence on many younger jazz players.

JULIAN BREAM and **JOHN WILLIAMS** are two of the most well known guitarists of today. Bream, who is also a lutenist, has had works written for him by, among others, Britten, Tippett, Walton, Henze and Malcolm Arnold. The Australian-born Williams, a pupil of Segovia, has premiered pieces by Takemitsu, André Previn and Stephen Dodgson. His interest in the guitar extends beyond the classical repertoire and into the fields of popular and folk music, where he has made several recordings.

LEFT: AN EXAMPLE OF AN EARLY VENETIAN GUITAR BY MATTEO SELLAS. NOTE THE INTRICATE ORNAMENTATION OF THE TABLE AND SOUNDHOLE.

above, largely to accompany. It was played with a plectrum and had metal rather than gut strings. Its frets, too, were of metal like those of the modern guitar; elsewhere they tended to be of gut and tied around the fingerboard. Sometimes it had courses of three strings.

✵ Notation Systems
The Alfabeto

As the Renaissance gave way to the early Baroque, so the four-course guitar yielded increasingly to the conventional five-course type. The first printed music for it had been published in 1554, in Spain, in Miguel Fuenllana's *Orphenica lyra*. It assumes an instrument tuned like the modern guitar but without its lowest string. A year later another Spaniard, Juan Bermudo, mentions a variety of tunings, but Fuenllana's reappears in the *Guitarra española* of Juan Carlos Amat, published in Barcelona in 1596. Here the *A* and *D* courses are tuned in octaves, the rest in unison. This was to remain, with little variation, a standard tuning throughout the Baroque period. To yet another Spanish theorist we owe the system of tablature known as *alfabeto*, which appears in the first manuscript source of music for the five-course guitar compiled by Francisco Palumbi in the 1590s. In this, chords are identified by letters of the alphabet. Of great significance is the fact that the system employs a series of vertical lines to indicate either an upward or downward stroke of

𝄞 LEFT: GUITARIST AND LUTENIST JULIAN BREAM HAS BEEN THE DEDICATEE OF A NUMBER OF WORKS BY SOME OF THE LATE 20TH CENTURY'S MOST EMINENT COMPOSERS.

𝄞 RIGHT: AN EARLY 18TH CENTURY GUITARIST AS DEPICTED BY THE ARTIST ANTOINE WATTEAU.

THE HARP-GUITAR WAS A CURIOUS HYBRID POPULAR IN ENGLAND IN THE EARLY 19TH CENTURY. IT WAS DEVELOPED BY EDWARD LIGHT IN 1798 AND IMPROVED BY HIM AS THE HARP-LUTE IN 1811 (ALSO SEE PAGE 41).

THE GREAT SPANISH VIRTUOSO GUITARIST ANDRES SEGOVIA HAD A PHENOMENALLY LENGTHY CAREER BEFORE THE PUBLIC, MAKING HIS DEBUT AT THE AGE OF 14 AND STILL PERFORMING INTO HIS EIGHTIES.

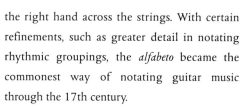

the right hand across the strings. With certain refinements, such as greater detail in notating rhythmic groupings, the *alfabeto* became the commonest way of notating guitar music through the 17th century.

By the mid-century, the five-course guitar was in general use in Italy, England and France as well as Spain. In Italy, music for it using *alfabeto* notation had been published as early as 1606 and found its first important native exponent in the person of Giovanni Foscarini, who worked in Italy and the Netherlands and published several books of *Intavolatura di chitarra spagnola*, not all of which have survived. The most renowned Italian guitarist of the succeeding generation is Francesco Corbetta, who published his first guitar music in 1639 and later settled in Restoration London as court guitarist to King Charles II. It was through Corbetta that the guitar in England achieved enormous popularity which played its

THE *Guitar Repertoire*

APART FROM THE THREE CONCERTOS BY THE ITALIAN MAURO GIULIANI (1808–20), THE MAJOR WORKS IN THE REPERTOIRE REFLECT OUR OWN CENTURY'S ACCEPTANCE OF THE GUITAR AS A CONCERT INSTRUMENT.

RODRIGO By far the most popular work – the *Concierto de Aranjuez* – is, fittingly, by a Spaniard: the Valencian Joaquin Rodrigo. It was first performed in 1940 and was followed by the *Fantasia para un gentilhombre* (1955) for guitar and orchestra, written for Segovia; the *Concierto Andaluz* (1967) for four guitars and orchestra; and the *Concierto-madrigal* (1968) for two guitars and orchestra. Rodrigo himself is not a guitarist, but writes idiomatic music imbued with the essence of his native country.

CASTELNUOVO-TEDESCO The Italian-American Mario Castelnuovo-Tedesco wrote two concertos (1939 and 1953) and a concerto for two guitars and orchestra (1962). He also wrote a series of 24 preludes and fugues in all keys for two guitars, *Les guitares bien temperées* (1962), modelled on Bach's *Well-tempered Clavier*. His Serenade for guitar and orchestra (1943) was another piece inspired by Segovia.

PONCE The Mexican Manuel Ponce, whose output consisted mostly of songs and works for piano and guitar, made a notable contribution to the guitar repertoire with the *Concierto del Sur* (1941), also written for Segovia.

BRITTEN Several leading British composers have been attracted by the guitar, mostly through the artistry of particular players. Benjamin Britten wrote his *Nocturnal*, based on a theme by Dowland, for Julian Bream in 1963. Six years earlier he wrote a cycle of *Songs from the Chinese* for voice and guitar.

WALTON The song cycle *Anon in love* by William Walton was written for Bream and Peter Pears in 1959. In 1971 Walton completed a set of *Bagatelles* for solo guitar, also for Bream.

TIPPETT In 1983 Bream gave the first performance of *The blue guitar* by Michael Tippett.

MALCOLM ARNOLD and **LENNOX BERKELEY** have written concertos for guitar; Arnold's dates from 1959, Berkeley's from 1974.

STEPHEN DODGSON has written several *concertante* works, most recently the *Duo concerto* for violin, guitar and orchestra of 1991. Although not a guitarist himself, he has produced a substantial number of chamber works featuring the instrument, some of the more recent for Nicola Hall.

own part in the decline of the lute. Corbetta had also been active in France, where the first tutor for the guitar was actually the work of a Spaniard – Luis de Briceño's *Metodo mui facilissimo para aprender tañer la guitarra a lo Español* (1626). The French Baroque school was brought to a peak of excellence in the music of Corbetta's pupil, Robert de Visée.

USUALLY PLAYED BY A STANDING MUSICIAN, THE FLAMENCO GUITAR IS LIGHTER THAN ITS STANDARD CLASSICAL COUNTERPART.

✄ The Making of the Modern Guitar

It was in France that the guitar was to metamorphose into the instrument we know today. Where courses were tuned in octaves, the lower note was known as a *bourdon* (*bordón* in Spanish). Around 1750 bourdons on the two lowest courses began to be accepted as the norm. At the same time it abandoned vestiges of so-called re-entrant tuning, where the pitches of the courses did not necessarily ascend or descend in sequence. The distinction between *punteado* and *rasgueado* lost some of its earlier significance as both styles were by now well and truly merged in guitar music. At this point tablature started to give way to staff notation, which established the modern practice of treating the guitar as a transposing instrument, its music written in the treble clef an octave higher than it sounds. The guitar, in fact, was losing its image as a specifically treble instrument, especially when a sixth course was added, tuned a fourth below the previous lowest.

Progressively the idea of courses was abandoned, leaving an instrument with six single strings such as we have today. Resistance to this survived until the early 19th century in Spain, no doubt as a reaction to the ultimate irony that a country to which the instrument had been 'imported' was now keen to sell back the improved model. Some of the principal tutors of the period are also by Spaniards; for example, the *Escuela de guitarra* by Dionysio Aguado (1825). By the second half of the century several modifications had taken place to produce what is essentially the modern guitar. These include the replacement of gut frets by fixed metal ones, the raising of the older,

𝄢 THE FENDER STRATOCASTER ELECTRIC GUITAR IS REGARDED AS THE STRADIVARIUS OF ITS TYPE AND IS FAVOURED BY MANY TOP ROCK MUSICIANS, INCLUDING ERIC CLAPTON.

STEEL OR HAWAIIAN GUITARS. UNLIKE STANDARD ELECTRIC GUITARS THEY ARE NOT HELD BY THE PLAYER.

lower bridge and the introduction of internal strutting in a radial or fan-shaped pattern instead of the former cross-struts. Credit for some of these innovations must go to Spain, notably to the father of the modern guitar, Antonio de Torres Jurado to whom a host of subsequent Spanish makers owe a debt of gratitude. Torres increased the size of the guitar, standardizing the vibrating string length at 65cm (26 inches) and facilitating the modern playing position in which the instrument is supported on the player's left knee. With this playing position the *apoyando,* or sweep of the hand across the strings, was free to emerge as a characteristic of guitar technique.

The renewed interest in the guitar from the late 19th century onwards has taken the Torres developments as its starting point. Chief innovations since 1945 have included a preference for nylon strings and an increasing interest in electronic amplification. The bass guitar which is commonly met with these days may seem like a new idea, but in its acoustic form dates back to experiments made in late 16th Italy in fitting the five-course guitar with a second neck carrying seven bass strings. Other bass instruments, with a single neck, were made in the 18th century. The modern bass guitar, invariably an electric bass, is tuned like the double bass (see page 26).

The electric guitar is not solely the preserve of the rock band. Several classical composers have exploited its sonorities, among them Michael Tippett in his opera *New Year* (1988). 𝄢

Related
INSTRUMENTS
℘

STEEL OR HAWAIIAN GUITAR
An electrically amplified instrument which stands horizontally on a tripod in front of the player. The sound is produced by means of a slide, operated by the left hand, to alter the sounding lengths of the strings. The instrument became popular in the 1930s when its characteristic *glissando* tones gave spurious ethnic flavour to Western dance music.
HARP-GUITAR/LUTE The first had eight gut strings running over a neck slightly shorter than that of the conventional guitar; a later model had 11 strings with the lowest four unfretted. The special feature of the harp-lute was its second neck, connected by a forepillar similar to a harp's. Most of the strings have only one fret, raising the pitch by a tone; a key at the back of the instrument raises it a semitone. The back was usually flat, enabling the instrument to be placed on a table to be played (see illustration on page 38).
UKELELE Developed from the *machete,* a small guitar introduced into Polynesia by the Portuguese. The word is Polynesian for 'jumping flea'. A *ukelele* usually has four strings, and tuning can vary. Its music is normally written in tablature.
BANJO Possibly originating in Africa, this round-bodied instrument consists of a skin or vellum resonator and has five strings. Early types are unfretted. Like the *ukelele,* the *banjo* is primarily an accompanying instrument. Hybrid *ukelele-banjos,* strung like the former but shaped like the latter, also exist.

♪ RARE STRINGS

THE GROWING INTEREST in period performance has brought about a situation in which virtually no instrument can be said to be obsolete. Nevertheless, a number of instruments now revived to serve the music originally written for them remain infrequent visitors to the concert hall, among them both bowed and plucked strings. There also exists a distinct group of instruments which attempt to combine the characteristics of both.

℁ *Viola d'Amore*

Pride of place in the first category goes to the viola d'amore, an instrument which owes allegiance to both the violin and viol families. When it was first reintroduced to the public in the 1950s the contention was that its name should be 'viola d'amor' ('viola of the Moors'), indicating that it had entered Europe via the Moorish invasions of Spain. This suggestion was supported by the shape of the soundholes in the face of the instrument: 'flaming swords', an Islamic emblem. But the date of the end of the Moorish occupation of the Iberian peninsula, 1492, gives too great a hiatus before the earliest known reference to the instrument. This is dated 1679 and appears in John Evelyn's Diary which, written in London, puts the presumed Spanish invention of the instrument at some time in the mid-17th century. In fact, there is no evidence for the instrument's Spanish origin. Its invention further north, perhaps in Germany, is indicated.

The viola d'amore retains the flat back and sloping shoulders of the viol, but is played on the shoulder like a conventional viola and lacks frets. Early models sometimes had only five

strings, later ones seven, although tuning was by no means standardized, with players adopting a *scordatura* appropriate to the key of a piece. Nevertheless, a common later tuning is *A, d, a, d', f sharp, a', d''*. Its chief attraction, however, is the presence of so-called sympathetic strings. These are not bowed but, tuned an octave higher than the main strings, resonate 'in sympathy' with them, giving a sweet and rather delicate sound.

As the name, which means 'love viola', suggests, the viola d'amore is one of several d'amore instruments. Another of this type is the oboe d'amore, which was prized in the late Baroque period for its special tonal quality as a solo rather than an orchestral instrument, not least as an *obbligato* instrument in vocal works. As such it features in several cantatas by J. S. Bach as well as in his *St. John Passion*, where two viole d'amore are deliciously paired with a lute. Its popularity

♪ A RARE CONCERT APPEARANCE BY THE BARYTON, IN THE HANDS OF JANOS LIEBNER, ONE OF A TINY BAND OF PROFESSIONAL BARYTON PLAYERS.

appears to have been highest in the German-speaking countries. Georg Philipp Telemann used it together with oboe d'amore and flute in a concerto, and parts for it are found in operas by his North German contemporaries Reinhard Keiser and Johann Mattheson.

The repertoire greatly diminishes after the mid-18th century, although there survive concertos by Karl Stamitz, a talented viola and viola d'amore player, and chamber works by him and his contemporaries. Thereafter its use in the 19th and early 20th centuries was as an isolated special effect, again more often than not in the opera house. Giacomo Meyerbeer wrote for it in *Les Huguenots* (1836), as did Puccini in *Madama Butterfly* (1904) and Janáček in *Katya Kabanova* (1921) and *The Makropulos Case* (1925). Taking the instrument's name literally, Janáček even considered using the viola d'amore instead of the viola in his second string quartet *Intimate letters* (1928), which was inspired by his unrequited passion for Kamila Stösslová.

By the beginning of the 20th century the viola d'amore had joined the growing ranks of older instruments then enjoying revival. One notable outcome of revival rather than survival is the *Kammermusik No. 6* (1927) of Hindemith, for viola d'amore and chamber orchestra. Hindemith also wrote a sonata for viola d'amore and piano, Op. 29/2, in 1929.

℁ *Baryton*

The baryton is really a larger version of the viola d'amore, held between the knees like a true viol, which enjoyed some popularity in the later 18th century. It has six bowed strings and up to 40 sympathetic strings. Joseph Haydn's patron Prince Nikolaus Esterházy was a gifted executant, and Haydn himself is known to have played the instrument. Haydn left several *divertimenti* which use the instrument.

✄ *Viola Bastarda*

This is a true viol, identical with the instrument known in England as the 'division viol'. It developed in Italy in the late 16th century as a smaller version of the bass viol and, as its English name suggests, was used for playing elaborate *divisions*, or variations, on existing melodies. Another name for it is the lyra viol, so called because it is played 'lyra-way'; ie, from tablature rather than from staff notation. This cross-fertilization between viol and lyra may account for the somewhat insulting name which this innocent instrument is given here.

✄ *Pochette*

Another group of bowed instruments is more directly related to the violin family. The pochette or kit violin is, as its name implies, a portable 'pocket-sized' instrument, particularly favoured by dancing-masters, and by street musicians, shepherds and others for whom the slim shape and diminutive size of the instrument proved handy. Although some specimens resemble genuinely small violins, the pochette is generally boat-shaped and has only three strings. These are the instruments designated as *violini piccoli alla francese* in the opera *Orfeo* (1607) by Monteverdi. Stradivari made a *kit* in 1717 which resembles a grotesquely stretched violin. Others were straight-sided from base to tuning pegs.

THE DIMINUTIVE POCHETTE OR 'POCKET FIDDLE', THE HANDIEST RELATIVE OF THE VIOLIN FAMILY.

℅ *Violino Piccolo*

The true violino piccolo is pitched a minor third higher than the violin. Its most celebrated use is in the first 'Brandenburg' concerto by J. S. Bach. Bach also wrote for a violoncello piccolo in some of his cantatas; there is a concerto in C for it by Giuseppe Sammartini. This instrument may be identical with the viola pomposa required for the sixth of his suites for solo cello. This is tuned like an ordinary cello but has a fifth string, sounding the *e′* above the *a* string. Some authorities, though, have claimed that the viola pomposa was an instrument played, like the viola proper, on the shoulder, whereas the violoncello piccolo was held like an ordinary cello but was of a smaller size.

℅ *Mandolin*

Of those instruments which are plucked, the mandolin is the best known and, at least as an amateur's instrument, has never really fallen into disuse. It takes its name from its shape; the Italian *mandolino* means 'little almond'. The mandolin's fingerboard is fretted like a guitar's and its tuning is identical to the violin's. The strings, however, are of wire and arranged in four pairs, each pair being tuned to the same note. This allows for one of the most characteristic features of mandolin playing, and the instrument's most effective way of sustaining a sound, the rapid *tremolando* between two notes of the same pitch.

From time to time the mandolin has attracted the attention of serious composers. Vivaldi wrote a concerto for two mandolins and another for one. Mozart used it in two songs of 1781: *Die Zufriedenheit* (K349) and *Komm, liebe Zither* (K351). His best known use of the mandolin is to accompany Don Giovanni's serenade *Deh, vieni alla finestra* in the opera of the same name (1787), a picturesque piece of scoring duplicated in the operatic repertoire's other *Barber of Seville* (1782), the one by Giovanni Paisiello. Even Beethoven, as a young man, produced two small-scale sonatas for the instrument. The mandolin was also the instrument taught to the young Paganini by his father.

℅ *Arpeggione*

The arpeggione was the invention of Georg Staufer of Vienna in 1823. This violoncello-guitar, as he called it, sought to combine the characteristics of the two instruments. Resembling a small cello, it possessed the six strings and fretted fingerboard of the guitar but was held between the knees and bowed. Its chief virtue lay in its extended compass and facility in playing full chords, together with the guitar-like effect of its *pizzicati*. It did not prove popular. Although the cellist Vincenz Schüster published a tutor for the instrument, it might have died virtually at birth had not Schüster prevailed upon Schubert to write a sonata for it. This work, D821, written in November 1824, has passed into the repertoire of cellists and violists. Arpeggiones have survived, though, to enable us to fulfil Schubert's – and Schüster's – original intentions. 𝄡

THE MANDOLIN, NAMED FOR ITS SHAPE, AFTER THE ITALIAN FOR 'LITTLE ALMOND'.

Except in the case of the double bass, changes to the modern string family have been relatively few since the 18th century. This is not to deny that occasional attempts have been made to take a completely fresh approach, as in the case of the acoustically rational instruments produced in France by François Chanot and Félix Savart in the 1820s. The former proposed a violin of almost guitar-like shape, completely curved and with long, narrow soundholes, while Savart's instrument was near triangular and not unlike the modern balalaika in appearance.

More conventional in design is the New Violin Family developed in recent years by the American Catgut Acoustical Society. This comprises eight instruments, the smallest being pitched an octave higher than the violin and the largest (shaped like a large cello) of the same pitch as the double bass. The standard violin is retained as, after a fashion, are the viola and cello, but these last two are of a size which complements their pitch relationship to the violin and to each other. Consequently the viola, known as the alto violin, is larger than its orthodox counterpart and has to be played between the knees like a cello. The cello itself, again larger, is called the baritone violin.

In addition, there is a soprano violin, pitched an octave higher than the alto; a tenor violin tuned an octave lower than the violin proper; and a bass violin with tuning a third lower than that of the baritone.

RIGHT: THE VIOLIN OCTET OR NEW VIOLIN FAMILY, ACOUSTICALLY MATCHED VIOLINS CHARACTERIZED BY THEIR TONAL HOMOGENEITY.

INDEX
STRINGED INSTRUMENTS

Stringed Instruments

The publishers would like to thank the following sources for their kind
permission to reproduce the pictures in this book:

AKG London, Arbiter London/Fender, Scottsdale, Arizona, Catgut
Acoustical society, Jean-Loup Charmet/Collection G. Harambourg, Paris,
Christies Images, Corbis, Mary Evans Picture Library, Maureen Gavin
Picture Library, Hulton Getty/Auerbach, Lebrecht/Maeder, National Trust
Photographic Library, Performing Arts Library/Clive Barda,
Popperfoto/Richiardi/ Roberto Serra, University of Edinburgh/Collection
of Historic Musical Instruments

Every effort has been made to acknowledge correctly and contact the
source and/or copyright holder of each picture, and Carlton Books Limited
apologises for any unintentional errors or omissions which will be
corrected in future editions of this book.